V4C 4V8

HEROIN

Helen Cothran, *Book Editor*

David L. Bender, *Publisher*
Bruno Leone, *Executive Editor*
Bonnie Szumski, *Editorial Director*
Stuart B. Miller, *Managing Editor*

An Opposing Viewpoints® Series

Greenhaven Press, Inc.
San Diego, California

Library of Congress Cataloging-in-Publication Data

Heroin / Helen Cothran, book editor.
     p. cm. — (At issue)
   Includes bibliographical references and index.
   ISBN 0-7377-0473-X (pbk. : alk. paper) —
   ISBN 0-7377-0474-8 (lib. : alk. paper)
     1. Heroin habit. 2. Heroin habit—Treatment. I. Cothran, Helen.
II. At issue (San Diego, Calif.)

HV5822.H4 H45 2001
362.29'38—dc21

                                                              00-057295

© 2001 by Greenhaven Press, Inc., PO Box 289009,
              San Diego, CA 92198-9009

              Printed in the U.S.A.

Table of Contents

Introduction

A man retrieved a package of white powder from his back pocket, removed a small quantity of it with the edge of his pocket knife, placed it on a pocket mirror, and began sniffing it. He had done this many times before in the restroom at his workplace, so he was focused calmly on the drug as it surged through him, bringing him instant relief from pain and anxiety. Moments later, however, he blacked out and tumbled to the bathroom floor.

The overdose didn't kill him; in fact, it probably saved his life. It forced him to enter into a treatment program for drug addiction. He got clean, got addicted again, got clean, got addicted again, got clean. This man did not grow up in a poor neighborhood where junkies shoot up on the streets and drug dealers kill each other in turf wars. This man came from the suburbs. He went to several of the best colleges in the country, got a high paying job working with computers, got married, had kids. He also joined an ever-expanding list of people who get addicted to heroin.

The great jazz musician Charlie Parker was a heroin addict. So was the blues singer Billie Holiday. Rock stars Janis Joplin and Kurt Cobain were both heroin junkies. Keith Richards, Eric Clapton, Iggy Pop—all at one time were heroin addicts. In 1996, Jonathan Melvoin of the rock band Smashing Pumpkins died from an overdose of heroin. The list of famous junkies is not limited to rock stars; the actor Robert Downey Jr. is currently serving a prison sentence on heroin-related charges, and William Cope Moyers—the son of renowned journalist Bill Moyers—is a recovering heroin addict.

Statistics show that heroin use since 1992 is on the rise in the United States, and many new users between the ages of twelve and seventeen come from the suburbs. In the period between 1980 and 1995, first-time heroin use for this age group increased fourfold. According to Join Together—a drug education organization—the over-all estimated number of heroin users increased from 68,000 in 1993 to 325,000 in 1997. Heroin use by twelfth graders increased by more than 100 percent from 1990 to 1997. The number of heroin-related cases in hospital emergency rooms throughout the nation increased by 64 percent between 1988 and 1994.

There are many theories to explain the rise in heroin use. Some attribute the drastic rise to new forms of heroin consumption: Heroin now comes in forms that can be sniffed or smoked, alternatives to injection that appeal to young people who see them as healthier and safer than injection. However, users who frequently consume the drug using these methods eventually use injection because as they develop a tolerance for the drug, injection gives them a bigger "rush" for their money. The Drug Enforcement Administration (DEA) has another explanation for the increase in heroin use. The DEA claims that "international drug traffickers have made a strategic marketing decision to push heroin as an alternative to cocaine" once cocaine use went down as a result of public information campaigns about its dangers. Richard Lowry, a political reporter for *National Review*, argues that heroin's rising popularity is due to the development of "grunge" culture. Since heroin is a drug of "isolation and oblivion," it appeals to young people eager to rebel against the broken—and increasingly middle-class—families from which they come. Karen Schoemer, reporting for *Newsweek*, observes that heroin has become high fashion. From musicians to fashion models, the stars that many young people look up to are using the drug. Says model Zoe Fleischauer, "There are a lot of junkies in the [fashion] industry. It's very hush-hush. . . . They wanted models that looked like junkies. The more skinny . . . you look, the more everybody thinks you're fabulous."

Even though current fashion may seem to raise the reputation and alter the method of consumption of heroin, the nature of the drug has not changed over time. According to the National Institute on Drug Abuse, heroin is a highly addictive drug. It is both the most abused and the most rapidly acting of the opiates, a class of drugs that also includes morphine and codeine. Heroin is processed from morphine—the legal drug doctors prescribe to patients in extreme pain—which is derived from the seed pod of certain varieties of poppy plants. It is usually sold as a white or brownish powder or as the black sticky substance known on the streets as "black tar heroin." (Other street names for heroin are "smack," "horse," and "junk.") Heroin was originally developed in an effort to find drugs that could help people overcome addiction to opiates, but it was quickly discovered that heroin was more addictive than morphine, and the drug was made illegal.

Despite the fact that heroin use has been illegal for decades, the drug today is more fashionable, purer in form, easier to obtain and easier to use than the drug of earlier days. Heroin today still exacts the same high price on the user, however: addiction and its personal and social costs. Even though heroin sold on the streets today is purer than in the past, it can still be cut with poisons such as strychnine that can put users in extreme risk. Overdose presents a persistent danger, and many overdoses result in death. Other health risks associated with heroin use are the contraction of AIDS and Hepatitis B due to the use of unsterilized needles, malnutrition, collapsed veins, bacterial infections, abscesses, infection of the heart lining and valves, arthritis, and rheumatological problems.

Not all of the consequences of heroin abuse are physical in nature. Heroin addiction also exacts a high price on the addict's family. Parents may feel shocked and betrayed when they discover that a child is addicted to heroin, and many blame themselves. Families can also feel the financial strain of addictive behavior as the addict spends an ever-increasing portion of household money on heroin. Individuals battling heroin addiction can lose their jobs as well, and some turn to crime in order to get money to buy the drug

In spite of the many individual costs associated with its use, people continue to use heroin for the way it makes them feel. Heroin causes people to feel warm and content, and it relieves stress. The Institute for a Drug-Free Workplace reports that heroin gives the user a short-lived state of euphoria, followed by drowsiness. It slows the heart rate, breathing, and brain activity, and depresses appetite, thirst, reflexes, and sexual desire. It also increases tolerance for pain.

Users must use higher and higher doses of the drug, however, in order to attain the same effect. Eventually, addicts inject the drug not to obain pleasure but to relieve the pain that sets in as the drug wears off. These withdrawal symptoms usually occur four to eight hours after the last dose and include chills, sweating, runny nose, irritability, insomnia, tremors, and body pain.

Treatment for heroin addiction takes many forms, but always requires stopping the use of heroin entirely. Since withdrawal from heroin "cold turkey" entails extreme pain, other treatments have been developed. The latest treatment for heroin addiction—Rapid Opiate Detoxification—allows a physician to anesthetize the addict so that he or she is unconscious during the most painful period of withdrawal. A more traditional approach to the treatment of heroin addiction is to replace the use of heroin with the use of methadone, another opiate, but one which does not have the same dangerous side effects as heroin and allows the user to live a relatively normal life. Most heroin treatment programs treat addiction as a health problem, not a criminal or moral problem; some even call heroin addiction a disease, but that contention is contested by others who see such labels as relieving the addict of responsibility for his or her addiction.

Heroin addiction also adds to the tremendous social burden imposed by illicit drug problems in general. Public Health Policy, a public health organization, estimates that in 1989, there were 10,710 deaths directly resulting from drug consumption in the United States. The total costs of illicit drug abuse were estimated to be $66.9 billion in 1991. Some of this cost is incurred due to medical treatment for addiction and physical illness as a result of drug abuse, and to drug education. A larger portion of the expense, however, is borne by law enforcement efforts which include interdiction, policing, judicial proceedings, and finally, incarceration. Public Health Policy claims that there are over 1.6 million people in prison on drug-related charges—many of those incarcerated are heroin addicts—and that the number keeps growing.

Anyone who snorts heroin at work knows firsthand the costs of drug addiction. He or she could face the possibility of prison, loss of family, job, and health; overdose followed by death is a constant threat. Maybe he or she could switch to methadone or get clean—in prison, in a treatment program imposed as an alternative to prison, or possibly without help—and begin living a productive, healthy life. The health and prosperity not just of rock musicians, models, and actors, but of ordinary people depends upon the quality of the discussion about heroin and the drug policies that arise from it.

1

The Lucrative International Heroin Trade

James Emery

James Emery is a journalist and anthropologist who has followed the drug trade in the United States and overseas for fifteen years.

The international heroin trade is extremely lucrative. Nations such as Afghanistan and Serbia smuggle heroin into Western Europe and the United States in order to raise money for warfare. Smugglers often justify their illegal activities by claiming that the money they earn is needed to fund important religious or political causes; such arguments are hypocritical, however, because drug trafficking goes against the laws and religious values of the countries which the smugglers claim to serve.

Much of the heroin that ravages human lives and society in Europe's inner cities arises paradoxically in Afghanistan, a nation of strictly enforced Islamic laws where drugs are banned by scriptural edict.

The powerful narcotic flows from its Afghan source in two meandering rivers: a northerly one through Uzbekistan, Tajikistan, and Turkmenistan and thence to Russia, Ukraine, the Baltic states, and Belarus before arriving in Europe and then partly being sent on to the United States; and a southerly one that stretches west to Turkey and then up through the Balkans and into western Europe's underground markets.

Most of Afghanistan today is controlled by the Taleban, a religious and military movement that sprang up a few years ago and quickly swept aside a gaggle of squabbling factions that had carved the country into fiefdoms.

Originating in dismal Pakistani refugee camps during the Afghan-Soviet conflict, the Taleban grew during the Afghan civil war between rival political factions following the Soviet departure. Its leaders, trained in fundamentalist Islamic religious schools funded by Saudi Arabia, promised to bring peace to an Afghan population weary of 16 years of warfare. The Saudis provided financing, and Pakistan supplied military training, weapons, and thousands of volunteers.

The Lucrative International Heroin Trade 9

On September 27, 1996, Taleban forces overran Kabul and imposed their highly restrictive version of Sharia, or strict Islamic law, which included numerous rules not explicitly sanctioned by the *Qur'an*, the Muslim holy book. The Taleban have forbidden women to work or attend school and enforced *purdah*, or mandatory veiling. Women are required to be covered head to toe with a *burqa*, a tentlike garment with a small, woven screen over the eyes.

A reign of terror overtook Kabul and other Afghan cities. Religious police from the Ministry for Promoting Virtue and Preventing Vice prowled the streets looking for lawbreakers. Playing music, singing nonreligious songs, or reading anything published outside Afghanistan became illegal. So is flying a kite, because it might interrupt prayers.

While the Taleban [who now rule in Afganistan] strictly enforce religious law, they quietly support their movement by dealing in drugs—despite a . . . ban on mind-altering substances.

The Taleban have their religious police," says Lois Gochnauer of the U.S. State Department's Human Rights Division. "They've been known to beat some women if their ankles are showing or if they are walking with a male who is not a close relative."

Men or boys wielding car antennas, electrical cord, or wooden clubs often do the beatings on the spot.

Zena, or illegal sexual intercourse, will result in 100 lashes before a cheering crowd of onlookers. If either party is married, the crime is worse. Adultery is a capital offense requiring *rajim* (death by stoning). The accused will be blindfolded, placed in a hole up to his chest, and stoned, with the entire village encouraged to participate. The victim's children, if any, are placed at the front of the crowd to see the consequences of their parent's crime.

In scenes reminiscent of the Roman Coliseum, Kabul Sports Stadium packs in capacity crowds of 30,000 to witness amputations, floggings, and executions. Murderers are killed, thieves have their right hand and left foot amputated, and other lawbreakers are flogged. Taleban soldiers enthusiastically parade around the stadium brandishing severed limbs as they stir the crowd to a frenzy.

Drugs and the Qur'an

While the Taleban strictly enforce religious law, they quietly support their movement by dealing in drugs—despite a Qur'anic ban on mind-altering substances. Opium has been a traditional crop in the "Golden Crescent"—Afghanistan, Pakistan, and Iran for centuries. At a 10 to 1 reduction ratio, opium is converted into heroin at remote labs scattered throughout the region.

U.S. Drug Enforcement Administration reports show that Afghan opium production dropped to an estimated 415 metric tons in 1990. But by 1997, under Taleban rule, over 2,800 metric tons were cultivated, a sevenfold increase.

According to U.S. government sources, the Taleban impose taxes on people who grow, refine, or transport opiates—opium, morphine base, and heroin—thereby generating a windfall of up to $50 million a year. The movement's drug taxes bought weapons and paid troops to conquer Afghanistan and are currently financing the Taleban's civil war against recalcitrant groups in the northern provinces.

Surveys conducted by the United Nations Drug Control Program (UNDCP) show that opium cultivation increased from about 49,000 acres in 1992 to over 155,000 acres in 1998. An estimated 200,000 farmers are involved. The UNDCP estimates that 40 percent of the raw opium on the international market in 1999 was grown in Afghanistan—96 percent from areas under Taleban control.

Afghanistan has received over $1 billion in international aid since the Soviets left 10 years ago. The 1999 UN budget called for $53.6 million in food aid, in addition to money for fertilizers and irrigation. Critics charge that UN food subsidies enable farmers to grow opium instead of traditional crops such as wheat, barley, and vegetables, and that fertilizers and irrigation programs are being used to increase opium yields.

The Taleban desperately want international recognition and have promised to help eradicate opium cultivation over an unspecified period in return for a seat at the United Nations. They also want several hundred million dollars in additional aid.

"The United States does not recognize the Taleban as the legitimate government," says Sheldon Rappaport, a State Department Afghanistan analyst. At present, only Pakistan, Saudi Arabia, and the United Arab Emirates recognize the Taleban government.

Sherman Hinson, policy planning coordinator with the Bureau of International Narcotics and Law Enforcement Affairs (INL), is cautious about Kabul's promises.

The Balkans provide a traditional heroin pipeline between Southwest Asia and Europe.

"Afghanistan is the second-largest producer [of heroin] after Burma," says Hinson. "The UN and U.S. attitude is: We'll be pleased to try and help you get rid of the opium but only after we see some persuasive evidence that you've taken the political decision to get rid of the crop. As yet, we haven't seen that."

The smugglers' routes

Hundreds of processing labs are located along the eastern border with Pakistan and in the north, adjacent to Uzbekistan, Tajikistan, and Turkmenistan, the primary transit routes out of Afghanistan.

"Heroin leaves Afghanistan by a variety of different routes," says Hinson. "Some connect with the long-established traditional routes of the Golden Crescent. Heroin then moves through Turkey and the eastern Mediterranean to the Balkans and what they call the 'Balkan routes' into Europe."

During the last few years, smugglers developed new routes through the former Soviet republics in Central Asia. UN sources claim that up to 65 percent of all Afghan opium and heroin is transported along these routes to the Baltic states, Belarus, Russia, and Ukraine on the way to lucrative European markets. The Russian mafia is heavily involved.

The Serbian government allegedly became involved in heroin trafficking to pay for wars in Bosnia, Croatia, and Kosovo.

"Organized crime, including money laundering," Hinson notes, "is one of the biggest problems facing Russia today. There are some pretty good, documented incidents of banks that have fallen into criminal hands." The DEA estimates that up to 25 percent of commercial banks in Moscow are controlled by organized crime.

The Balkan connection

The Balkans provide a traditional heroin pipeline between Southwest Asia and Europe. According to the United Nations, up to 60 percent of illegal European hashish, heroin, and morphine base originates in Afghanistan and is smuggled along the Balkan route. Ethnic Kosovar Albanian drug traffickers are second only to the Turks as the predominant heroin smugglers along this popular passage.

The original Balkan route runs from Turkey to Bulgaria to Yugoslavia. The southern route extends into Albania, Macedonia, and Greece. The northern route, which resurfaced during the civil war in the former Yugoslav republics, travels through Bulgaria, Romania, Hungary, Slovakia, and the Czech Republic. Heroin abuse has increased in all these countries as a result of transit spillover.

Drug smugglers have taken advantage of weak east European economies to bribe poorly paid police and customs officials.

"Corruption is a major problem in eastern Europe," says Brian Furness, INL program officer for eastern Europe, "and it is having a serious impact on governing institutions and economic institutions." Foreign investment and joint ventures are suffering because of the perception of corruption.

"Everywhere," Furness continues, "the drug trade is a major contributor to corruption. It makes governing a lot more difficult."

Criminal syndicates operating out of Turkey and Europe have used Serbs, Albanians, and the Kosovo Liberation Army (KLA) to transport heroin and other narcotics. Both forces use drug profits to buy weapons. Yugoslavia, comprising the former republics of Serbia and Montenegro, remains a popular drug transit route. In addition to overland routes north, the Adriatic Sea provides smugglers with links to Italy.

The Serbs and Albanians are involved in smuggling cigarettes, drugs, guns, and illegal immigrants. Both groups have long-standing ties to Italian criminal organizations. Albania and Serbia have refused to sign any international drug control treaties despite growing activity by local criminal elements.

The Serbian involvement

The Serbian government allegedly became involved in heroin trafficking to pay for wars in Bosnia, Croatia, and Kosovo. According to World Geopolitics of Drugs (OGD), an international monitoring agency based in France, three Serbian state organizations are directly linked to the drug trade: the Interior Ministry Secret Police, the Foreign Ministry Information and Documentation Service, and the Counterespionage Service. Former secret service networks dealing in drugs are virtually immune to prosecution.

Zeljko Raznatovic, alias "Arkan," formerly connected to the Croatian military counterespionage unit, is reputed to be heavily involved in the drug trade and arms shipments. He is wanted by Interpol but is welcome in Serbia. Arkan and his men were known for their brutality and excesses in carrying out ethnic cleansing in Bosnia and Kosovo during the mid-1990s.

"There's a problem with the turbulence that has happened since the breakup of old Yugoslavia," says the INL's Hinson, "particularly since the imposition of sanctions on Serbia spurred almost industrial-scale smuggling activity for the purpose of breaking the sanctions. Once somebody does business with contraband smuggling of that type, any form of contraband is just so much grist in the mill."

Serbian criminals use immigrants in Italy to smuggle drugs and other contraband. Claire Parangelo with the State Department's Italian Desk told a reporter, "The Serbian immigrants are engaging in organized crime in general in the north of Italy. There are many Serbs in the Venice-Trieste-Milan area, so there is a lot of networking up there. The Albanians are primarily in the south of Italy."

The Albanian network

This latter group, working through ethnic Albanian enclaves throughout Europe, makes up one of the largest criminal operations on the entire Continent. Some KLA members are running heroin to Kosovar Albanians in Germany, Austria, Switzerland, and Sweden, using profits to buy arms and finance their activities against the Serbs.

If you have an organization smuggling heroin, you increase your profit margin by sending [smugglers] who want to immigrate, instead of using "mules" as couriers that have to come back.

Over the last five years, hundreds of opulent mansions belonging to Albanian mafiosi and independent drug dealers have been built near ports along the Adriatic coast.

"Would I be shocked to find that people in the KLA are involved in drug trafficking in some way, either to make money or by telling themselves they've got a cause where the end justifies the means?" Hinson mused. "I'd be shocked to find out it wasn't true. It's tremendously easy for anyone who wants to be a bandit just to claim that he's a partisan."

The Albanians buy weapons and heroin from criminal groups in Russia and the former Soviet republics. The heroin is transported and sold into Italy and west Europe. The profits pay for the weapons.

Albanian smugglers, using speedboats called *scafi*, run heroin and illegal immigrants between Albania and Italy, earning $75,000 to $100,000 a trip. In addition to drugs, they can carry 50 to 60 passengers, each paying a few hundred dollars to be smuggled into Italy. The passengers, primarily ethnic Albanians, but also Kurds and Pakistanis, seek employment opportunities.

The Sacra Corona Unita, a group of Italian mafiosi, is directly involved in Albanian smuggling operations. "That's the organization that dominates Apulia, in the heel of Italy's boot," says the INL's Furness. Several other criminal groups also deal with Albanian and Serb smugglers. More powerful Mafia-type organizations are the Dramgheta, based in Calabria; the Sicilian Mafia; and the Camorra in Naples. "They're economic," adds Furness. "Smuggling drugs is part of what they do."

"Smuggling people into Italy is still an enormous problem," says Parangelo. "The criminal groups are especially from Albania and the former Soviet Union. If you have an organization smuggling heroin, you increase your profit margin by sending people who want to immigrate, instead of using 'mules' as couriers that have to come back."

Most of these criminal groups are not single-purpose but are poly-crime organizations. If they are into smuggling contraband, they'll smuggle the contraband that brings them the highest profit margin, be it cigarettes or drugs.

The drug trade is complex. Traffickers may be deemed criminals, celebrities, or freedom fighters, depending on what cause they support and who is doing the judging. Regional conflicts and civil wars provide both the incentive and opportunity for smugglers, often wearing the mask of patriotism and making stupendous profits at the expense of thousands of lives.

Afghanistan and the Balkans are just two links in this undulant, invidious trade—a transnational, transoceanic serpent that eventually buries its teeth deeply in a significant minority of Europeans, rending the social fabric of the Continent.

2

Rockers, Models and the New Allure of Heroin

Karen Schoemer

Karen Schoemer is a senior writer at Newsweek. *She previously wrote a monthly music column for* Interview *and* Mirabella *magazines.*

Heroin is becoming increasingly fashionable—especially among young people—for a variety of reasons. One reason for heroin's rising popularity is that the drug is more widely available, cheaper and purer than in the past. Another reason for its popularity is that heroin can now be snorted or smoked, methods of consumption that appeal to casual drug users who mistakenly believe they won't get addicted unless they shoot up. One of the primary reasons that heroin's reputation has soared, however, is the rise of heroin use among icons in the fashion and music industries. Although there have always been heroin addicts in the rock music industry, rock stars have become heroin junkies in increasing numbers. Young people—who idolize rock stars—try to emulate them by using heroin. Images in books, magazines, and movies about heroin addiction, and the punk and alternative rock movements have encouraged teenagers to use heroin in order to be cool, tough, and rebellious. Despite its cool image, however, heroin often leads to addiction, overdose, and, sometimes, death.

I never tried heroin, but I used to think I wanted to. White and middle class, just out of college in 1987, I read Jim Carroll's *The Basketball Diaries*, a cornerstone of modern heroin mythology: he made it seem like the ultimate rite of passage, a drug that made you funnier, wiser, cooler and full of hilarious stories about running wild on New York's Lower East Side. I listened obsessively to the Rolling Stones' "Exile on Main St." and read accompanying literature like Stanley Booth's *The True Adventures of the Rolling Stones* that told how strung out Keith Richards was during this peak of genius. I even knew someone, a musician, who did heroin. For a long time he didn't do it around me. I nagged him to let me try it, and he laughed. "You're not starting," he said.

When he finally did use it around me, my romantic image of heroin collapsed. He nodded out on my couch midway through a sentence; he threw up in my bathroom; he went face down on a restaurant table in front of my friends. From then on, I *hated* heroin. When at last he offered it to me, holding a knife point piled with ivory powder under my nose, I backed away. "I thought you wanted to try it," he said. "Not anymore," I said. Now I'm old enough to know better. I have a husband and a house and a nice life. When I hear that a musician I admire uses it, I'm concerned but no longer curious. When I hear of a tragic rock overdose, like Jonathan Melvoin of Smashing Pumpkins, I feel sad and shake my head, just like anybody would. I can enjoy a heroin movie like *Trainspotting* and all the while I'm secretly thinking: Whew! Glad it's not me!

Yet no matter how smart we think we are, heroin's allure persists. In the past two or three years, its presence in pop culture has risen dramatically. Maybe it's Kurt Cobain's fault. His was the most high-profile drug-related rock-star death since the '70s, and he was battling heroin when he committed suicide in April 1994. Maybe it's his wife Courtney Love's fault: her torn dresses, matted hair and bruisey demeanor put a fashionable spin on junkie chic. Maybe it's the rock world's fault. In the past few months Smashing Pumpkins drummer Jimmy Chamberlin, Stone Temple Pilots singer Scott Weiland and Depeche Mode frontman David Gahan have all been busted for heroin and/or cocaine. (All three pleaded not guilty; Weiland and Gahan entered rehab.) Aerosmith could be the latest drug-troubled band: they just fired longtime manager Tim Collins, an anti-drug crusader credited with helping singer Steven Tyler and guitarist Joe Perry get off heroin in the mid-'80s. Sources say Tyler may have relapsed this year. *Newsweek* has obtained a copy of a pained letter the band wrote to Tyler in June, citing his childishness, negativity and denial. The band members threatened to break up Aerosmith, telling Tyler to "get the help that you need" and "reach out" for counseling. The band is said to have spent weeks with Tyler at Steps, a treatment center in California. Tyler denies all this. "I'm still sober and have remained sober for the last nine years, going on 10," he says. "Sometimes the creative zone and *joie de vivre* I get into throws people. If that's what they see in me, so be it, but I'm as sober as I'll ever be." Collins hopes Tyler *is* clean. "Steven's an icon of recovery," he says. "If he dies of an overdose, the people around him are going to be in big f—ing trouble."

No matter how smart we think we are, heroin's allure persists. In the past two to three years, its presence in pop culture has risen dramatically.

The resurgence is Hollywood's fault, too. Quentin Tarantino revived John Travolta's career when he cast him as a dope fiend in *Pulp Fiction*. (And we got to watch Uma Thurman's lips turn overdose blue.) *Trainspotting* a techno-color trip through Scotland's junkie underbelly, is the most hyped film import of the summer. Actor Robert Downey Jr., so effective on screen as a druggie in 1987s *Less Than Zero*, got busted in June for coke and heroin possession, arrested in July when he wandered into the wrong house and now resides in a lock-down detox center. (He's pleaded not guilty to the June charges.) CAA, a top agency, has dropped three clients because of alleged drug use, including Downey.

Meanwhile, there have been growing complaints about "heroin chic" in fashion. Designer Jil Sander drew flak when her catalog showed a druggy-looking woman with one sleeve pushed up. Waif extraordinaire Kate Moss has made a career out of looking wasted. Model Zoe Fleischauer, 21, developed a heroin habit almost immediately when she moved to New York three years ago, and she says she wasn't alone: "There are a lot of junkies in the industry. It's very hush-hush." Now clean, she blames the fashion world for glamorizing the problem. "They wanted models that looked like junkies," she says. "The more skinny and f—ed up you look, the more everybody thinks you're fabulous."

What all this cultural noise means is that heroin is back up from the underground. Back in the '80s, higher prices, lower purity and the AIDS crisis fear of needles kept it out of the mainstream. Part of the resurgence is simple economics: heroin is now cheaper and purer, and the volume being imported into the country has doubled to around 10 to 15 metric tons since the mid-'80s. Abundant supplies of high-grade blends attract everyone from hipster rock stars to Wall Street executives to inner-city addicts. A new government report scheduled for release this week will show that overall drug use among those 12 to 17 years old has risen almost 80 percent since 1992 (page 57). Baby-boomer parents may be shocked by the new casual attitude toward heroin, which even in the drug days of the '60s carried a stigma that seemed to set it apart from pot, acid and the Summer of Love.

But alternative rock has its roots in the punk movement, not the hippie era. When Nirvana's 1991 album "Nevermind" hit No. 1, a range of attitudes and behaviors from the fringe of pop culture suddenly hit the mass market: dressing rebelliously, flouting conventions, screaming real loud, taking drugs if you want to. The most revered bands carry out the message in their lives as well as their songs. Since kids emulate rock stars, they're liable to emulate their drug use. The number of top alternative bands that have been linked to heroin through a member's overdose, arrest, admitted use or recovery is staggering: Nirvana, Hole, Smashing Pumpkins, Everclear, Blind Melon, Skinny Puppy, 7 Year Bitch, Red Hot Chili Peppers, Stone Temple Pilots, the Breeders, Alice in Chains, Sublime, Sex Pistols, Porno for Pyros, Depeche Mode. Together these bands have sold more than 60 million albums—that's a heck of a lot of white, middle-class kids in the heartland. Bob Dole is making drugs a Presidential campaign issue in 1996. How long is it going to take him to turn on MTV.

The music business, it seems, is already anticipating an attack. Ten years ago cocaine was so widespread that one former label executive reports getting hired after doing a line in the president's office. Today attitudes have changed. Ask executives if there's a heroin problem in the music business, and more than one will answer, "Absolutely." "It's worse than it's ever been," says one record-company vice president. Art Alexakis, singer for Everclear, has been drug-free for 12 years, but he still has to deal with other bands' problems. "I've walked into my dressing room and had people sitting on my amp, shooting dope," he says. "That was two years ago, when we were still at the opening stage. They wouldn't shoot up in their own dressing room, being the headliner. They'd come over to our place."

Mike Greene, the head of The National Academy of Recording Arts & Sciences, which puts together the Grammy Awards, is leading the charge by pushing an outreach program called MusiCares. Last December and again in June, he called together 400 members of the industry for closed-door symposiums to discuss the issue. The idea is for executives, managers and agents to stop looking away when an artist clearly has a drug problem. "It's a moral question," says the label vice president, "and we don't like to talk about morality and rock and roll. But the f—ing right wing does, and if we don't clean our own house, then we become vulnerable to them."

Abundant supplies of high-grade [heroin] blends attract everyone from hipster rock stars to Wall Street executives to inner-city addicts.

This moral question has deeply shaken the music business. Judging from some of the responses to Greene's initiatives, the industry is far from a consensus on how the problem should be handled. Many musicians are suspicious of the executives' motives. "They don't want their artists taking dope because they won't be able to milk more platinum out of them next season," says singer Henry Rollins. Even among executives, bitter factions are emerging. Conspicuously absent from Greene's symposiums were key members of Kurt Cobain's management team, John Silva and Danny Goldberg of Gold Mountain. (Goldberg is now the president of Mercury.) In the wake of Cobain's suicide, former Aerosmith manager Collins, who is closely allied with MusiCares, wrote a save-our-artists editorial in Billboard magazine that implicitly accused Cobain's people of allowing him to die. Neither Silva nor Goldberg will discuss the situation publicly. But Ron Stone, another manager at Gold Mountain, responds angrily. "I find it the height of hypocrisy that people run around grabbing headlines about how they're going to do all these things," he says. "The reality is, none of the record companies are going to let go of a platinum artist because they're on drugs. And if they would take a position saying 'We don't want to do business with you,' then there's 20 other record companies that would do it in a second."

At the heart of this conflict is anguish and guilt over Cobain. Two and a half years later, emotions remain raw over his loss. Cobain was like the star pupil at a high school full of promising young talent. He was a brilliant musician and a nice person. No matter how many Pearl Jams, Stone Temple Pilots and Bushes reach the top 10, he can't be replaced, and his decision to commit suicide has left a terrible pall over the industry. "We constantly tried to get him help," says Stone. "The truth is, when he sobered up, when he made a serious attempt to get his life in order, he took a real good look at his life and he killed himself."

Despite all this, heroin's rep soars. People mistakenly think that it's not addictive if they snort it or smoke it. "In L.A., people are doing it on a real casual basis," says Rollins. "Like, 'Oh, me and my girlfriend did heroin this weekend.' Like it's a trip. Like it's a vacation. And I'm looking at them, going, 'Are you out of your f—ing mind?'"

The fear is that the drug is becoming just another trend. "You got a million needles tattooing kids," says singer Exene Cervenka. "You got a million needles piercing their ears, piercing their noses, piercing their lips. You got a million needles shooting drugs into their veins. And to them it's all the same thing. I don't think kids can differentiate between behaviors." The streets of Seattle are cluttered with kids who've moved there to do heroin, just because Cobain did—and this at a time when people in the Seattle music scene claim drug use among musicians is tapering off. Singer-songwriter Paul K, who's been clean for six years, finds the "I have to do it because Keith Richards/Lou Reed/Kurt Cobain did it" excuse pretty lame. "It's like buying Paul Newman's salad dressing," he says. "Have you tasted it? I mean, it's not very good." But even he admits the power of a junkie idol. When did he start using? "Probably the day I put down *The Basketball Diaries*."

Unfortunately, cool images in books, movies and magazines don't jibe with the reality of addiction. While Sid Vicious was being mythologized as junk's favorite casualty in the '80s, Sex Pistols guitarist Steve Jones was strung out on the streets of L.A. "I lost everything, financially and emotionally," he says. "Lost *everything*. I was literally walking up and down Hollywood Boulevard with one pair of jeans and one pair of tennis shoes, looking to steal a handbag off some old lady to get another fix." With the help of a 12-step program, Jones cleaned up 12 years ago. And even when the images are negative—*Trainspotting* conscientiously focuses on the drug's *un*glamorous side—the degradation can be part of the appeal. "It has to do with being young and self-destructive," says Tim Foljahn of Two Dollar Guitar, who quit using three years ago. "It's got the reputation as the meanest, dirtiest drug—which I would not necessarily agree with, because I've seen them all destroy people. But it's got that death tag on it. It's as bad as you want to get."

> *The fear is that [heroin] is becoming just another trend.*

And once someone is addicted, it doesn't matter who he is. "An addict is an addict," says Dave Navarro, guitarist for Red Hot Chili Peppers. Clean for four and a half years, Navarro used heroin while in Jane's Addiction, an influential first-wave alternative band. But he started long before that. "When my mother died when I was 15, I discovered I didn't feel it as badly when I was loaded." People speculate that the pressures of success and touring contributed to the deaths of Cobain and Shannon Hoon of Blind Melon, but Navarro says it works the other way around. "In Jane's Addiction I felt very unsure, very uncomfortable," he says. "By the time we were successful I was so down in the depths of despair that I didn't experience any of it. Perhaps the level of success we did reach enabled me to get through the destructive side of my use quicker, because I was able to spend more money and go down faster. Whereas who knows how many years it would have gone on had my habit been $50 a day?"

Recovery has allowed Navarro to see his addiction in clear terms. "Heroin ruined my dreams," he says. "It made my work life an unhappy experience. Basically turned the one thing that I had worked my whole life for into the thing I wanted to get away from most." He tried to detox several times before entering a long-term rehab program after Jane's Addiction broke up in 1991. "Being in the Chili Peppers, I'm able to experience what I'm doing," he says. "I'm able to be present for it. And happy with what I'm doing for the most part. I would never trade that feeling for anything in the world. It's a long road, but it's well worth it. At least it was for me."

Some L.A. musicians in need of recovery turn to Gloria Scott. A 67-year-old former beatnik, biker chick, hippie chick and junkie with fluffy blondish hair, thick round glasses and dentures that click when she chews gum, Scott is the kind of person a cool, tough, rebellious rocker could connect with, because she's cool, tough and rebellious herself. Her war stories could make any self-obsessed 27-year-old look like a wimp. In the '60s she lived across the canal from Jim Morrison in Venice Beach, and Morrison used to put his head on her pregnant belly and listen to her son, Solo, moving around. In the '70s she and jazz drummer Buddy Arnold, now a bigwig at Musician Assistance Program, ran a scam trading phony prescriptions for pharmaceutical heroin. She got clean 17 years ago, and works as a counselor at Socorro, a treatment center in East L.A. She can't name the young musicians who've come to her, due to the tenets of the 12-step program but she understands their plight. "I don't think it makes any difference if it's Keith Richards or Kurt," she says. "They're all idols. It sounds romantic, it's gloom and doom, it's like a secret organization. Then it gets ugly. You've got a band you love, a career you love, but *this comes first.*"

Scott helps take some of the scariness away from getting well. She doesn't preach the 12-step program; in fact, she doesn't mind pointing out some of its flaws. "I hated being clean," she says. "Hated those goddam meetings," she says. "We'd go to Beverly Hills, and these women all had sport coats and long f—ing nails. I said, 'Give me a break! I wouldn't use with people like this. Why would I get clean with them?'" She had an additional problem with recovery: she doesn't believe in God. When she was told to focus on a higher power, she tried to think of something that was bigger and stronger than she. First she decided on Neil Young, who sang the anti-junkie anthem "The Needle and the Damage Done."

Later, she chose the ocean. Sometimes Scott walks along the Venice boardwalk, past apartments and alleys where she used to shoot up and deal drugs, and the memories don't bother her. The water nearby takes her out of herself. She doesn't swim in the ocean. She hasn't since she got sober. She's learned a lesson that many young musicians are still struggling with. When something's more powerful than you, it's best to stand back and leave it alone.

3

Teen Heroin Abuse Is a Serious Problem

Eileen Moon

Eileen Moon is a freelance writer from New Jersey.

Heroin use in the United States has increased, especially among teenagers. Heroin overdoses by teens quadrupled in the period between 1980 and 1998, and emergency room visits due to heroin abuse increased by 64 percent. Heroin abuse is no longer only a problem in poor minority communities; increasingly, white, middle-class teenagers from the suburbs are becoming heroin addicts. The drug's rise in popularity can partially be attributed to the fact that heroin can now be snorted, a method of ingestion that is falsely perceived by young people to be less dangerous than injection. Another reason for its popularity is that heroin is now viewed as "glamorous" because some models, rock musicians, and Hollywood stars use it. Heroin use among young people today has serious consequences: It can lead to painful withdrawals, and to the transmission of infectious diseases such as AIDS if injected. Heroin use can also result in overdose, and sometimes, death.

In a precedent-setting move in July 1998, authorities in Texas arrested 29 people and charged them with complicity in the deaths of four Plano, Texas teenagers who died of heroin-related overdoses. In a 36–count indictment, the defendants were accused of knowingly distributing the illegal drug to the young people named in the indictment despite their knowledge that the drug could kill them. Each of the 29 people indicted were identified by authorities as contributing to the deaths of 20–year-old Milan Michael Malina, 19–year-old George Wesley Scott, 18–year-old Robert Lowell Hill and 16–year-old Erin Baker.

The arrests were the result of a painstaking, step-by-step investigation launched by Plano Police Chief Bruce Glasscock and federal law enforcement officials in September 1997. Over the course of 1998, the dragnet took officials from the homes and schools of Plano to the border of Mexico.

Reprinted from Eileen Moon, "The Horse They Rode Out On," *Professional Counselor,* December 1998. Reprinted with permission from the author.

The case was the first of its kind in the Eastern District of Texas, where state law does not allow drug dealers to be charged with murder as a result of a drug overdose.

But with federal enhancements of Texas drug statutes, the defendants may face up to 20 years in prison for their roles in bringing the drug from Mexico to the United States, distributing it to local dealers, or selling the substance directly to those who died as a result of ingesting it.

To many who have witnessed the terrible epidemic that has claimed the lives of more than a dozen young people in the Plano area since 1996, it is clear that drug dealers are targeting the young people in this affluent area of Texas as a prime market without regard for the tragedies they are causing.

One man indicted in the law enforcement dragnet was McKinney, Texas, resident Salvador Pineda Contreras, 26, who admitted to authorities that he acted as a distributor of heroin for an associate who sent a courier to Mexico each weekend to pick up a supply. Authorities reported that Contreras showed no remorse, saying that the deaths caused by the drug were "not his problem."

It is a problem, however, for all who care about the young people of Plano and other cities similarly under siege by the easy availability of heroin. Among them is Dallas social worker and substance abuse counselor, Lois Jordan.

Jordan, a counselor at Solutions, an intensive outpatient treatment program for alcohol and substance abusers, says she is on a mission to put a stop to the epidemic that is taking an average of more than one life a month in the affluent communities that surround her city.

The victims [of fatal heroin overdoses], largely, are young people between the ages of 17 and 20; kids from good neighborhoods; kids from good homes.

The victims, largely, are young people between the ages of 17 and 20; kids from good neighborhoods; kids from good homes.

Nevertheless, they're dying.

Early in 1998, 13 patients underwent treatment at Solutions. Eight of them were heroin addicts. Five of those eight were high school students. Two were college kids. One was a 28-year-old man.

All of them had taken a step toward recovery by entering treatment. But the danger for them is far from over.

It's as near as their next drink; their next joint; the next anything that will weaken their defenses and trigger their craving for heroin. When the drug of choice is heroin, one slip can be a fatal mistake.

And the fact that they're in treatment is no guarantee that Jordan and her colleagues won't be reading their obituaries in the newspaper one day soon.

Many of the hopeful faces staring out from graduation pictures that accompanied their obituaries in newspapers in Plano and Dallas, over the past two years had been in treatment, but slipped back—back into the party milieu that sent them on a short ride from a sip of champagne to a hit on a joint to that last, deadly snort of heroin.

Newspaper editorials have expressed outrage and concern; parents have responded in anger and grief to news that came too late—news that their kids have been living on the edge; that the unlucky among them had fallen over that edge in ways that ended their lives.

Once, heroin was a drug associated with the inner city; with poor, minority communities—with junkies "shooting up" in alleyways. But the downtown, dead-end drug has moved uptown in recent years, gaining a dubious respectability as it found favor with models, rock musicians and Hollywood stars—even as it took lives along the way.

Moving into suburbia, it claimed more victims among high school cheerleaders, churchgoers, football players, fresh-faced college kids.

"The first kid I lost to heroin was in 1987," says Jordan, a social worker who has been a substance abuse counselor since 1983. The boy who died was David Barnhill, a 20-year-old from Highland Park, a suburb of Dallas. The tragedy hit Jordan hard. More were to follow.

By 1998, the list of young lives lost to heroin in the Plano/Dallas area was swiftly approaching 20, averaging one a month throughout 1997 and 1998.

The epidemic wasn't occurring only in Texas. While some have pointed to the state's proximity to Mexico and the drug trafficking made easier since the United States relaxed trade barriers through the NAFTA [North American Free Trade Agreement], over the past few years heroin has been enjoying a renaissance among the young people throughout America.

Research compiled by the Partnership for a Drug-Free America reveals that first-time use of heroin by teenagers quadrupled from the 1980s to the 1990s. In 1995, there were an estimated 140,000 first-time heroin users in the nation—the great majority of them under the age of 26.

The deadliness of the drug is evidenced by the fact that heroin-related cases in hospital emergency rooms throughout the nation increased by 64 percent between 1988 and 1994.

In some areas, bodies were being dropped off at emergency room doors.

Heroin addicts often share a "junkie pride," in belonging to a special club, similar to that felt by gang members in the inner city.

That's where George Wesley Scott, a 19-year-old philosophy major at the University of Texas in Austin, ended up. While home in Plano for the summer, Scott went partying with some friends at a local motel. The partying included the snorting of chiva, a popular form of heroin that is mixed with antihistamines and snorted.

Scott, an asthmatic, stopped breathing. He was dead when his friends dropped him off at the hospital. But they didn't stay around to have that confirmed.

It's the ease of ingesting heroin by snorting that some credit to its image as a popular party drug. Unlike the grittiness of inner-city drug users who shoot up, suburban users can achieve the high without having to confront the similarities between their use of heroin and that of the back-alley junkie.

"These young preppy kids start using it because they can snort it," says Jordan. "A couple of girls I've worked with told me that for a week or two, guys would give it to them for free. Then they would start charging them $10 or $20 for it. By that time, they were hooked."

By the time they entered treatment, Jordan says, the girls' addiction had progressed to the point where they were injecting heroin three times a day.

The glamorization of the deadly drug in movies such as *Pulp Fiction* and *Trainspotting*, in music television videos and in glossy print ads for trendy clothes has added an edge of sophistication to heroin addiction.

"Heroin chic"—demonstrated by ads featuring thin, unkempt, sickly waifs with pallid skin photographed in stark black and white—caused an outcry in recent years as the drug took its toll among the famous and the obscure nationwide.

What was responsible for the terrible embrace that held the young people of the nation in the grip of heroin? How could it be stopped?

As newspapers and magazines began exploring the causes and possible cures, Jordan, too, was looking for answers.

What she found was surprising.

"I kept asking myself, 'Why is this yanking my chain? Why am I on a mission'?"

The answer had a lot to do with her own history, she realized.

A recovering alcoholic who has been sober for 17 years, Jordan is also the mother of an adult daughter who is herself a recovering alcoholic.

"I thought to myself, 'That's me, and if someone had introduced me to heroin, I know it would have done for me what booze did for me. It could have been me. It could have been my daughter.'"

Jordan sees a strong connection between the attraction that alcohol holds for alcoholics and the seductiveness of heroin for junkies. Both drugs create in the user a warm, mellow feeling, acting as an anesthetic for the uncomfortable feelings that erupt in real life.

Giving up an addiction—whether heroin or alcohol—requires "learning to live in your own skin," says Jordan.

The National Institute on Drug Abuse describes heroin as a highly addictive substance that is the most rapidly acting drug in the opiate family. Heroin is an extract of morphine, which is distilled from certain varieties of poppies.

The first commercial heroin was marketed by the Bayer Company of Germany as a cough remedy. For a time, it was a popular choice for surgical anesthetics, but doctors soon discovered that is was far more addictive than morphine.

In the early years of the twentieth century, the typical heroin addict was a white woman between 30 and 50; a housewife with children. "She may have ordered the family remedies from Sears & Roebuck," Jordan says.

Today's heroin is pedaled in several forms. "Black tar" heroin, is a black, sticky substance. Heroin also is sold as a brown or white powder that is mixed with sugar, starch, powdered milk or quinine. In some cases, heroin sold on the street has been mixed with strychnine or other deadly substances.

But the powerful drug needs no additional substance to make it deadly. Because a heroin user has no way of ascertaining the strength of a particular dose, any ingestion of heroin can prove fatal.

There are many other risks associated with heroin use, including the transmission of AIDS and other infectious diseases via the sharing of needles. The short-term effects of heroin are the production of a pleasurable sensation known as a "rush," depressed respiration, clouded mental functioning, nausea and vomiting, pain suppression, and spontaneous abortion.

Long-term effects include addiction, collapsed veins, bacterial infections, abscesses, infection of the heart lining and valves, arthritis, and rheumatological problems.

Parents have justified how they can drink and do certain things. Kids see that and are justifying their [heroin use].

While overdose can kill a heroin addict at any time, withdrawal is painful —so painful that many addicts believe that they will die. Experts say that won't happen, although a pregnant heroin addict may endanger her baby's life by going through withdrawal "cold turkey."

Why would anyone take the risks associated with heroin use?

For some personalities, says Jordan, risk-taking is what it's all about. "Living on the edge" has an intensity that appeals to those who are most susceptible to addiction.

The drug is said to have an "orgasmic" effect that ensnares users again and again. But the myth of heroin as an overpowering addiction different from all other addictions is just that, Jordan believes—a myth.

Unfortunately, it's a myth that plays right into the hands of the narcissistic, grandiose personality drawn to heroin addiction and convinced of their own "uniqueness."

Once over the shame that often accompanies the initial descent into addiction, heroin addicts often share a "junkie pride," in belonging to a special club, similar to that felt by gang members in the inner city, Jordan says.

The truth is that heroin isn't special at all.

"It's simply liquid alcohol," says Jordan. "It eases the pain and makes life more bearable."

It differs from alcohol in that it is not toxic to the liver, kidneys or other body organs. But withdrawal from heroin can be a journey through hell.

Several new drugs have been developed to ease withdrawal. Synthetic opiates like LAAM (leva-alpha-acetyl methadol), Naloxone and Naltrexone are some of the drugs that block the effects of morphine and other opiates, reducing the cravings they cause.

The most-well known pharmaceutical approach to heroin withdrawal is the use of methadone, which has been in use for more than 30 years. The problem with methadone is that it simply substitutes one addicition for another, critics say.

The bottom line is that heroin addicts, like all addicts, have to fully commit to recovery, making the changes in their lives that will ensure their sobriety. They must not drink—news that no heroin addict wants to hear, says Jordan.

Alcohol lowers the defenses that keep a heroin addict from using, Jordan says. In several instances in the past few years, the use of alcohol has preceded the fatal episode of heroin use that took the lives of young people in the Dallas area.

As with alcoholics, the grandiosity of the heroin addict knows no bounds. "This is a pretty affluent area, and we get a lot of people in our office thinking that they're unique," says Jordan. "I love to work with people like that because I put them in their place real quick. Tolerance has built up; loss of control is going on. I tell them 'You are going to have to realize that you are a precious person, but you are not unique. Part of the nature of addiction is wanting to be catered to and considered special.'"

Behind the heroin epidemic in Plano are sociological factors that are replicated in other towns across America.

Plano is an affluent, fast-growing community that has sprung up in response to the presence of large corporations in the area that have attracted employees from towns around the nation. One suburban high school in the area has 3,000 students. "There were 250 kids in my graduating class," Jordan says. In a school as large as 3,000 kids, it may well be impossible to feel at home.

"A community like this is lacking roots," Jordan says. "There are new families coming in. There is a lot of insecurity. There is a lot of social insecurity: people don't take a stand with one another and say, 'I saw your kid doing this.' There is a lot of instability in the family system."

And behind the attractive suburban doors, there is also a lot of alcohol abuse.

"What we have is a generation that has grown up where their parents are alcohol abusers or untreated alcoholics. The parents have justified how they can drink and do certain things. Kids see that and are justifying their behavior because they grew up in that situation. It's a lack of values and a lack of commitment to themselves. Parents want to point their fingers at their kids and not look at themselves," says Jordan.

The rising tide of heroin deaths has alarmed the community and alerted many to the need to establish the roots that have been missing. Churches and community groups are working together to address the problems lurking behind the luxuries of life in the new suburbia.

Some recent studies have shown that today's teenagers are more likely to identify heroin as a dangerous drug. There is hope that the deadly era of "heroin chic" is at an end.

And while addictions in one form or another will likely always be with us, the good news is that treatment, too, has moved into the mainstream.

"This generation is far more likely to seek help than their parents' generation," says Jordan. A generation ago, "You didn't let anybody know that something was wrong in your home."

4

The Press Exaggerate the Heroin Abuse Problem

Jack Shafer

Jack Shafer is the deputy editor of Slate, *an online magazine published by Microsoft Corporation.*

The heroin-related death of Jonathan Melvoin—of the rock group Smashing Pumpkins—and the release of the movie *Trainspotting*— a movie about heroin addicts—has prompted the press to publish a rash of articles announcing a new heroin epidemic. But the press have been announcing a "new" heroin epidemic for years. The media's obsessive coverage of heroin addiction is often overstated, contradictory, and misinformed. One newspaper reports the purity of heroin at 70 percent while another reports it at 30 percent, for example, while neither publication explains that levels of purity actually have little or nothing to do with overdoses. Alcohol used in combination with heroin does contribute to rates of overdose, but the press consistently underreports that finding. Furthermore, the press neglect to report government statistics that show that heroin use has actually declined.

In July, 1996, the press reprised one of its favorite stories: Heroin is back. The news hook was the July 12 death of Smashing Pumpkins side man Jonathan Melvoin, 34, while shooting scag in a Park Avenue hotel. The *Washington Post* Page One obit on Melvoin claimed—without substantiation—"a resurgence in heroin use in the '90s," while the *New York Times* asserted that the "heroin vogue has been building since at least 1993 and shows no signs of ebbing." *Trainspotting,* the 1996 movie about young Scottish junkies, provided another useful occasion for noting this alleged trend.

Always coming back

"Smack Is Back"? For the press, smack is *always* back. It never goes away, but it's always returning. Boarding the Nexis [article database service] wayback machine, we find that nearly every publication in America has sounded the heroin clarion yearly since 1989: the *New York Times* ("Latest Drug of Choice for Abusers Brings New Generation to Heroin," 1989); *U.S. News & World Report* ("The Return of a Deadly Drug Called Horse," 1989); the *San Francisco Chronicle* ("Heroin Making a Resurgence in the Bay Area," 1990); the *New York Times* ("Heroin Is Making Comeback," 1990); *Time* magazine (Heroin Comes Back," 1990); the *Los Angeles Times* ("As Cocaine Comes off a High, Heroin May Be Filling Void," 1991); the *Cleveland Plain Dealer* ("Police, Social Workers Fear Heroin 'Epidemic,'" 1992); *Rolling Stone* ("Heroin: Back on the Charts," 1992); the *Seattle Times* ("Heroin People: Deadly Drug Back in Demand," 1992); NPR ("Heroin Makes Comeback in United States," 1992); *Newsweek* ("Heroin Makes an Ominous Comeback," 1993); the Trenton *Record* ("A Heroin Comeback," 1993); the *Washington Post* ("Smack Dabbling," 1994); the *New York Times* ("Heroin Finds a New Market Along Cutting Edge of Style," 1994); *USA Today* ("Smack's Back," 1994); the *Buffalo News* ("More Dopes Picking Heroin," 1994); the Fort Lauderdale *Sun-Sentinel* ("Heroin Makes a Comeback," 1995); the *Times-Picayune* ("Heroin Is Back as Major Problem," 1996); the *Arkansas Democrat-Gazette* ("State Gets Deadly Dose as Heroin Reappears," 1996); *Rolling Stone* again ("Heroin," 1996); and the *Los Angeles Times* ("Heroin's New Popularity Claims Unlikely Victims," 1996).

For the press, smack [heroin] is always back. It never goes away.

The granddaddy of the genre appeared 15 years ago in *Newsweek* ("Middle-Class Junkies," Aug. 10, 1981), with language that reads as fresh today as it did then. We learn that heroin has breached its ghetto quarantine: "[C]hildren of affluence are venturing where once the poor and desperate nodded out. The drug is being retailed at rock clubs, at Hollywood parties, and among lunch-time crowds in predominately white business districts." As always, part of the problem is a glut of white powder: "[S]heer abundance is prompting concern about a potential 'epidemic' spilling across demographic divides." And heroin purity is increasing dramatically: "Purity levels as high as 90 percent have been found in seized wholesale caches, with street level purities averaging up to 20 percent—around six times the typical strength of the 1970 Turkish blend."

Purity and overdose

Having hit 90 percent 15 years ago, you wouldn't think that heroin purity could keep rising. But for the press, it has. The *Washington Post's* story about Melvoin reported that heroin purity has risen from "as low as 4 percent in past decades to upward of 70 percent today," while the *Los Angeles Times'* piece noted that heroin had gone "from 4 percent [purity] in 1980 to 40 percent in 1995." After Melvoin died, the Associated Press reported that the heroin he shot was 60 percent to 70 percent pure.

Depending on where you drop the Nexis plumb line you can find references to more potent street heroin in the recent past. A 1989 *New York*

Times story pegged the potency of heroin at 45 percent. In 1990, the *Washington Post* placed average purity at 30 percent to 40 percent. A *Seattle Times* story from 1992 quoted a Drug Enforcement Administration source who said that in the '70s, heroin was typically 25 percent to 30 percent pure, but that heroin seized in the early '90s was now topping the scales at 67 percent pure. A 1996 government study puts purity at 59 percent, so if the DEA was right a few years ago, recent purity actually has declined somewhat.

Another risk factor that never gets enough ink in the heroin-obsessed media is the danger of using heroin in combination with alcohol.

There is good evidence that potency isn't the most significant risk factor in overdose deaths. A study of heroin overdoses in Washington, D.C., the findings of which were published by the *Journal of Forensic Sciences* (1989), found no relationship between heroin purity and death-by-overdose or nonfatal overdose. (On the night that Melvoin shot that 60 to 70 percent heroin and died, Pumpkins drummer Jimmy Chamberlin shot the same junk and survived.) The researchers attributed most overdoses to intermittent or post-addiction use of heroin—meaning that people who OD'd tended to misjudge tolerance when returning to the drug. Another risk factor that never gets enough ink in the heroin-obsessed media is the danger of using heroin in combination with alcohol. The mixture has an additive effect: A drinker could spike himself with a lower-than-lethal dose and still OD.

Inadequate knowledge

What do we really know about heroin use? For one thing, the federal government's National Drug Control Strategy for 1996 says that the addict population is basically stable. It reports that the number of "casual users" (less than weekly) of heroin came down by nearly half between 1988 and 1993 (539,000 to 229,000), the most recent year measured, while the number of "heavy users" (at least weekly) dipped from 601,000 to 500,000. One statistic feeding the heroin "revival" stories is the increasing number of emergency-room visits by people who mention heroin as a reason for seeking ER treatment. But the statistics, which come from the government's latest Drug Abuse Warning Network (DAWN) survey, come with a disclaimer suggesting that the explanation may be multiple visits by aging druggies who are using the ER for a variety of health problems.

My bet is that when the medical examiner releases his report on Jonathan Melvoin, it will disclose that the smashed pumpkin was drinking booze while shooting, a fatal error that pre-'50s addicts almost never made. We'll learn that Melvoin—like the press—was an amateur who didn't really know what he was doing with heroin.

5

The Tragedy of Heroin Addiction

Curtis P. McMaster

Curtis P. McMaster is a primary counselor at the Institute of Human Development, a substance abuse rehabilitation center in Atlantic City, NJ.

Heroin addiction has serious consequences for the addict and society. For the addict, addiction results in desperation, deteriorating self-respect, and declining health. For society, addiction fuels the destruction of inner cities such as the ghetto in Philadelphia, where the illegal drug trade prospers in the midst of terrible poverty. The prevalence of addiction to heroin and other drugs in the United States has produced countless programs designed to prevent addiction or treat it once it occurs. These new methods of stemming drug abuse will save some people from the horrors of life-long addiction, but many lives and communities will continue to be destroyed because of drug abuse.

A glaring orange summer sun rises over the edge of I–95 as we flash past the acres of ocher squares that make up the Philadelphia panorama. The cityscape comes into our view, and the scene is transmuted by the sun's rays into a shimmering, surreal mural—a picture of eternal and flawless perfection.

But Duke and I can't appreciate the beauty. We are hurtling northbound, into the ghetto known as "The Badlands," against the onslaught of the withdrawal pains that will catch us if the day grows any longer. Duke is hunched over the wheel of our battered moving van, which doubles as a taxi for any [heroin] junkie who can put gas in the tank. I'm riding shotgun, mentally navigating the miles in an attempt to erase them.

Like countless other mornings, the trip feels more as if I'm running away than rushing to somewhere. It's impossible to remember how long I've been doing this, every day is exactly the same.

No words are spoken in the truck. We are too lost in misery to communicate and too intent on our mission to waste attention on anything else. The smell of our unwashed bodies mingles with the highway and

Reprinted from Curtis P. McMaster, "Out of the Badlands," *Professional Counselor*, June 1998. Reprinted with permission from the author.

industrial stench. Uncombed hair, dirty clothing and unshaven, sunken faces have become so standard we are long past embarrassment or concern.

I feel the searing pain of withdrawal knife through me. In mute agony I consider killing Duke and then myself—a desperation born of hatred and mercy. Our addiction to heroin has joined us to it and each other in a bond of utter hopelessness. Years of need and resentment lock us in the circling of gladiatorial slaves, where even the survivor loses.

It will be only minutes now. But fear turns these minutes into an eternity of expectation. We are parched travelers approaching an oasis that could be dry, but must not be.

It's business as usual. They see us coming.

"How many?" they ask.

"Four of poison," I respond.

In a smooth exchange, $40 goes out the truck window and heroin comes in. Two blocks later we pull over and take water from a dripping hydrant. A moment later we are sitting cross-legged in the rear of the truck, performing the daily ritual: mix with water, heat for a moment, draw into syringe, tie off arm and search for the least-damaged vein; insert needle and pray for that rich red gush that signifies success. Finally we inject it slowly, and close our eyes to contain the warm glow that has become the only thing in life worth saving.

Destination: Badlands

They call it "The Badlands." The heart of it is about a square mile of North Philadelphia ghetto. Much of it actually looks like a post-apocalyptic movie scene where civilization is a fading memory. Crumbling buildings sag and fall apart, lots are piled high with debris, scarecrow people with predatory looks live without heat or water in shells humorlessly called "abandominiums." The area's infamous reputation for its terrible poverty is secondary to its reputation for being the largest drug trafficking neighborhood in the area.

The largest employer [in the Philadelphia ghetto] now is the illegal drug trade.

Each day, all day, thousands of addicts trek into this urban jungle to search its gray tapestry for the flecks of crystalline white that have become the main focus of their lives. In the shopping sections, half the stores are boarded up and the other half eke out a living by catering to the needs of the desperately poor—used clothing and used furniture stores, dollar stores and bars. The factories that once provided some support to the area are long gone. The largest employer now is the illegal drug trade. The imperativeness of survival has created a multi-generational cottage industry, with kitchen tables for processing, street corners as distribution centers, and 14-year-olds for sales representatives.

Even the junkies are amazed at the brazen drug-dealing gangs who have taken over the street corners with a cold, casual aplomb denoting ownership. They hawk their brand names openly and loudly: "TNT! We got TNT bags! The best!" Each bag of heroin is stamped with the logo or name of the entrepreneurial association that distributes it: Homicide, Chevy, Poison—creative advertising is not limited to Madison Avenue.

The main conversation of Philadelphia-area addicts consists of which bag is the most potent of the day. Lines of cars, 10 and 20 deep, form at that corner, crawling past as routinely as if it were a fast-food drive-through. Paid lookouts guard the perimeter, ready to warn by shouting "5-0," the slang term for "police." Narcotics squads patrol constantly, but simply don't have the manpower to do more than momentarily slow down the machine.

Part of the reason for the big profits is the introduction of crack cocaine, the cheap new drug that gives an intense but only momentary high, followed by an insistent urge to feel the intensity again, and again. Synthetic heroin is another part of the equation. A hundred times stronger than organic heroin, its introduction to the streets has dropped the cost of production and transportation considerably. It is a short trip from a basement lab around the corner to the sidewalk merchant.

Carelessness in the cutting process sometimes causes a rash of over-doses and deaths until the batch is caught or sold out. The tragicomic results illustrate the depth of need and lack of common sense addiction is capable of—a lemming-like rush to distributors by addicts seeking the "killer" bags that can actually kill. Twice within recent months, tainted bags left addicts dead and sent hundreds to emergency wards, yet within hours it was business as usual. The selling locations were reopened a few blocks away.

Scenes that would prompt instant arrest anywhere else are so commonplace they are ignored in order to keep enough space open in the jails for violent criminals. Even seasoned police officers are forced into pragmatic choices. "I ask them to take their drug use inside," said one officer on national television, "so the children don't see." It's the best he can do.

"It wasn't always like this," a police lieutenant tells me. "When I was a young, skinny cop on the beat here 25 years ago, I had no idea this could happen. Drugs were pretty much small-time then. There was a known drug dealer that I left alone, solely for the purpose of using him to target the area's criminals for me. At the time, I considered that the best method to keep a check on crime in my district. One day the drug dealer joked with me and said, 'When I make a million, I'm going to retire.' A year later he closed up shop and left, and I watched as his employees took the business and spread like locusts over the whole neighborhood."

Problems and solutions

The '60s game of recreational drug use began in a carnival atmosphere of freedom and fun. But it became a firestorm that continues to rage, leaving behind images that are beyond chaos. Places like The Badlands are the all-too-visible evidence.

Business people snort cocaine at power lunches, school children take pills as if they were candy, housewives hand tranquilizers to their next-door neighbors, the neighbors gratefully send back joints in return, teenagers kill over a few feet of drug-selling territory, stoned and drunk drivers turn their vehicles into high-speed murder weapons.

Yet the quasi-acceptability of substance abuse has fostered an attitude of ambivalence. Many simply relegate it to that corner of the mind where social ills are filed. Is it the grand scale of the problem that evokes such apathy? Do media-spawned visions of Uzi-armed cartels freeze us into resignation? Or is it a more familiar presence that we fear—rubbing shoulders with it every day? The kid on the corner doing sleight-of-hand tricks? The next-door neighbor who sells a little coke on the side?

New Age thought, a trend toward life affirmation and personal growth, evolved as a backlash to the emptiness left behind when drug use burned a hole through the last three decades. This newly assembled wealth of knowledge, emphasizing the connection between mind, body and spirit, is filling the vacuum with positive thought, spirituality, fellowship, exercise and natural substances instead of drugs.

Every family in America can now claim a member with an addiction problem.

For those who found themselves sick and alone, addicted and disenfranchised, 12-step programs—the largest spiritual movement of this century—have become household words, as more people are discovering that there is no problem that won't surrender to the power of people helping people. In addition, programs like "Just Say No to Drugs," and "D.A.R.E." are empowering children by subtracting the peer pressure factor and adding education for positive, responsible decision-making skills.

We now know a great deal about this disease, and the enlightenment has been a long-awaited expiation for those who've been shackled by addiction. It is an illness as guiltless and real as any physical ailment, often a natural response to our worst social problems: dysfunctional family situations, violence and poverty. But this revelation has dimmed before its proliferation, and seems to have come in the eleventh hour.

Every family in America can now claim a member with an addiction problem, someone whose inability to quit leaves little room for sympathy as it mars the peace and happiness of the others. The blight of substance abuse has created a suffering society that is fearful, frustrated and simply longing—not for cures or apologies but for an end. Addicts, consciously or unconsciously, are also looking for an end. Peace or oblivion, it really doesn't matter which in the face of a lifetime of physical and emotional illness, beatings, rapes, starvation, imprisonment, lost relationships and little or no self-esteem or respect.

As a recovering heroin addict, all my thoughts and days have been spent searching for the answers to this most excruciating of sufferings. I know there is no easy path out of the netherworld for the addicted, or simple answers for society as a whole. But it is clear that we don't have a choice anymore. We must find them.

Survivors and victims

As I neared the end of this article, I wasn't sure how to close it. I stopped writing and telephoned Duke. We spoke in the language of gratitude that those introduced to the dimension of spirit understand. He was fishing from the deck of his home, which is on a marina in Palm Beach, Florida. He finished our conversation by saying, "Come visit me soon. Life's been good and it's getting better."

I walked out onto the patio of my home in rural New Jersey to enjoy the woodlands that I've become so attached to, and to reflect.

It is quiet here, except for a muted background of birds and the skitter of squirrels, who approach me and beg for seeds and nuts. As I step out to feed them, an earthy scent rises, the sun envelopes me, and something tells me that a measure of happiness is the inalienable right of every living being.

Gazing at the peaceful vista, I wonder at fate and ask it the same questions I always do. Is it a lust for life, or some benevolent cosmic entity that intercedes for the hopeless and lost? Can it be as simple as asking for help from a compassionate society?

What about the others—the thousands we have known, the millions yet to come? The ones who never made it out? Is there sanctuary for all those tortured and dying?

Or must they keep turning back, in futile movement, to the dark hope of The Badlands?

6

Parents of Heroin Addicts Undergo Emotional Distress

Jane Adams

Jane Adams is a Seattle-based writer whose most recent book is I'm Still Your Mother: How to Get Along with Your Grown-up Children for the Rest of Your Life.

Heroin addiction does not just affect the addict—it also affects the addict's family. An increasing number of affluent parents are having to cope with the knowledge that their adult children are heroin addicts as more young people discover that recreational use of heroin quickly turns to addiction. When parents learn of their child's addiction to heroin, they often react with disbelief, guilt, anger, and despair and need help coping with these emotions.

They sit together on the tweed couch in the crowded, overheated library of a brick and stucco church, a handsome, prosperous-looking couple in their late 50s. Her puffy, red-rimmed eyes dart around the room; he stares blankly at the ceiling, thinking how he'd rather be almost anywhere but here—in his office, on his boat, at his club, someplace where he's in command, in control. Finally, when the last person straggles into the library and the Nar-Anon meeting begins, Jim Thompson expels the breath he's been holding in. At least there's no one here he knows—a potential embarrassment that has concerned him since he told his wife, Sally, he'd come. It is the reason they passed up closer meetings and drove 20 miles from their San Francisco condo to this distant suburb.

Nar-Anon is to Narcotics Anonymous as Al-Anon is to Alcoholics Anonymous, a support group for friends and families of substance abusers. And how could Jim Thompson explain to those who know him as a successful businessman and civic leader something he doesn't even understand himself—his 24-year-old son's addiction to a drug Jim and Sally had never thought would touch their lives? "Alcohol, marijuana, even cocaine—I could understand those things," says Jim. "But heroin? That absolutely threw me for a loop!"

Reprinted from Jane Adams, "My Child on Heroin? Impossible!" *Reader's Digest*, April 1997. Reprinted with permission from the author.

"He's just taking a while to find himself," Jim had told Sally when Scott lost his third job in 18 months. "She wasn't right for him," Sally told Jim, when Scott's fiancée returned his engagement ring. "He says it's a sure thing," they told each other when they learned Scott had spent his $50,000 inheritance from his grandfather on what he assured them was an investment in a hot new Internet company. Jim's face crumples. "We knew he tried pot a few times and drank once in a while—most kids do. But he finished high school at the top of his class; he went to Yale. Heroin? I still can't believe it."

Heroin. To the Thompsons and their peers who grew up in the 1940s and '50s, the word itself conjures up ugly, unforgettable images— Lenny Bruce dying in a toilet stall, a wasted Billie Holiday being led away to jail, Frank Sinatra playing a struggling addict in *The Man with the Golden Arm.*

"We wanted to believe Scott—he always had a good explanation for everything that happened," says Jim. When Scott's ex-fiancée finally told Sally she'd broken the engagement because Scott refused to admit he had a problem, Sally was confused. "I said, 'A problem with what?'" Sally recalls. "And when she said, 'Heroin,' I thought she was nuts. Heroin is something people use if their life is so bleak and awful they want to end it, and Scott wasn't like that."

[My son] finished high school at the top of his class; he went to Yale. Heroin? I still can't believe it.

Even if they heard or read about heroin use among Generation Xers, most parents like the Thompsons associated it with a very different population—"those without hope," as Sally put it. But at the Nar-Anon meeting outside San Francisco, the very presence of so many 50-plus suburbanites whose children or grandchildren were addicted to the drug reflects the striking rise, nationwide, in the number of young adult heroin users.

From 1978 through 1994, according to the Drug Abuse Warning Network, hospital emergency-room admissions for heroin-related episodes jumped 80 percent, from 4,700 to 8,400, for 18-to 25-year-olds; the number climbed 400-plus percent, from 4,800 to 21,600, for 26-to 34-year–olds. Even more frightening, indirect markers like ER admissions and treatment-center figures tend to lag behind what's actually happening, and criminal-justice figures don't reflect the many well-to-do young addicts who are never arrested.

"They often start by 'nick-nacking around' at parties," explains Ron Jackson, director of Ever-green Treatment Services in Seattle. "They feel like it's not a problem, even though they know it's not good for them; for some it's a rite of passage, like overdrinking at frat parties. And heroin is effective for dealing with many life stresses at this age—anxieties about careers, money, one's love life."

"The scary part is that these kids don't have the heroin memory of an earlier generation," says researcher Wayne Wiebel of the University of Illinois at Chicago School of Public Health. "They see it as a relatively benign drug that produces a warm feeling, not as frenzied and overstimulating as cocaine, without the loss of control that comes with alcohol. What's more, they think they're not at risk by snorting or smoking it. This population doesn't relate to needles or addicts or dependency, not at first. But they're moving from smoking on weekends at parties to more regular use, with a rapid and dramatic increase in tolerance." As tolerance increases, Wiebel notes, so does the need to continually adjust the dosage upward to produce the same effect, and "eventually they overcome their aversion to needles."

At Nar-Anon meetings, parents often describe their heroin-addicted adult children as "so gifted," "so full of potential" or "so smart." Jim Thompson tells of Scott's nearly perfect SAT scores, his brilliant college career. "I asked him, 'How could someone as smart as you are get involved with a drug like this?' And he said, 'This drug was smarter than I am.'" Young people like Scott don't take heroin to get high; they take it to avoid the loneliness and despair they sometimes feel.

Carrie Meade, who discovered her 28-year-old daughter's addiction when she opened the powder-room door at a family Thanksgiving and caught Julie smoking heroin, downplays the despair factor. "Sure, every generation thinks it has it tougher than the one before," she says, "but my kid had everything going for her—a great job, a loving husband, a beautiful home."

But Julie tells a different story: "It was all a facade. Underneath, I was anxious, insecure and scared I couldn't live up to people's expectations of me. Heroin put me in this blissful, euphoric state, where all my doubts about who I was just drifted away."

> *I'm not guilty, I'm mad [about our daughter's heroin addiction]! . . . All that effort, energy and hard work, that love and caring we poured into her, and she throws it away.*

"These kids have been raised to expect the world to welcome them with open arms," says the father of a 22-year-old former National Merit Scholar who's a heroin addict. "When it doesn't, they turn to drugs as an escape." He shakes his head in despair: "Where did we go wrong?"

Blaming themselves is a typical and understandable reaction of many parents whose children use heroin. But drug-abuse counselors urge parents to focus on how they can help their loved ones recover rather than on what they might have done in the past. "Addiction is an illness, not a moral issue," says Nar-Anon literature.

While that offers some comfort, it's not always enough: "I'm not guilty, I'm mad!" says Carrie Meade. "All that effort, energy and hard work, that love and caring we poured into her, and she throws it away—pfft!—like that! If she had problems, if she was anxious or insecure, why didn't she tell us?"

Tell them? Most parents aren't in day-to-day contact with their adult children—often they see or hear from them only sporadically, and the effects of heroin use aren't always readily apparent.

"This isn't their problem, it's mine," said a 29-year-old computer engineer who's been heroin-free for three years; his employer's health plan paid for his month-long inpatient treatment. "I told my parents I was going to Europe on vacation, and I even had one of my friends mail them postcards. Eventually I'll tell them, because copping to your problem is part of the 12-step deal, but not until I'm sure I'm going to stay off drugs. Why should they have to suffer, too?"

The majority of parents interviewed for this article learned about their children's addiction firsthand. "My son lost his house, his job and his wife—when he hit bottom, he told us why," says one man. "In a hundred years, I'd never have believed it if I hadn't heard it direct from him. I went through all the classic stages of grief, from denial to acceptance. But there are still times I think, 'It couldn't be. Not my kid.' And then, sometimes, I cry."

"My daughter called me one night, bawling," reported the mother of a 30-year-old lawyer. "I asked, 'What's the matter? Have you lost your job? Did you have a fight with your husband? Are you sick?' And she said, 'I need treatment, but I can't use my job health insurance—they'd probably fire me.' I asked, 'Treatment for what?' When she said, 'Heroin,' I felt a knife go through my heart."

The anonymity requested by parents who spoke to New Choices reflects a special stigma attached to heroin addiction. "Even treatment centers demonize heroin," says Barbara Stern, a drug counselor in San Francisco. "That makes it harder to find quality help for this problem." When family members come to Stern, seeking information or assistance, she advises them to start with Nar-Anon and counsels that "if you think your adult child has a heroin problem but he—or she—says he's only used a few times and it's nothing serious, don't believe him. Once or even twice may be an experiment, but after that it's an addiction. Despite what some people say, there's no such thing as a weekend junkie."

If an adult child doesn't want to stop and resists help, there's not much a parent can do, says Stern. "If I had the money and my kid wanted to stop, I'd opt for Betty Ford or another high-quality center, where he'd be with his peers. But I'd make the cost of the program a loan, not a gift. And the second time I wouldn't pay a nickel; I'd refer him to a local public program, make him face the consequences of the addiction and cut him loose." Remember, she tells parents, "It's not the responsibility of any treatment program to cure your addict, just treat him, care for his medical problems, point him in the right direction and provide aftercare and monitoring. And it's not your responsibility, it's his."

Stern urges parents to attend meetings at Nar-Anon or similar groups for emotional support and to utilize other public and private community resources. "You can help your kid by expressing love and understanding," Ron Jackson advises parents, "refusing to support the habit or a lifestyle that promotes it, and being supportive of interventions you might not like, such as methadone."

Says Carrie Meade, "Julie always seemed so strong and on top of things. She's clean and sober now; last week we celebrated her second-year anniversary off drugs. She's even planning to have a child soon. I don't regret a penny of the money I spent to help her get well, but I miss the sense that I could take her health and happiness for granted, the way I always used to. Maybe that was blind of me, but it was wonderful while it lasted."

7
Treatment for Heroin Addiction

Join Together

Join Together is a community support organization that creates action kits about drug abuse that encourage a broad array of groups and individuals to take action on timely issues affecting their communities.

The various treatments for heroin addiction fall into two categories: drug and nondrug treatments. Once detoxification has occurred in which the patient gradually adjusts to being heroin-free, either or both treatments can commence. Of the drug treatments, methadone is the most widely prescribed. This treatment uses methadone as a substitute for heroin because methadone satisfies the addict's craving without causing the harmful side effects associated with heroin use. LAAM (levo-alpha-acetyl-methadol) is used like methadone, but LAAM has the benefit of lasting longer than methadone. Both Naloxone and Naltrexone counteract the effects of heroin and help prevent relapse. Nondrug treatments include contingency management therapy and cognitive behavioral intervention. Contingency management acts on a reward system: Recovering heroin addicts are subjected to regular drug tests, and if their tests are negative, the patient receives rewards such as items that promote healthy living. Cognitive-behavioral interventions try to change the addict's thinking and behavior. Ideally, both drug and nondrug therapies should be used concurrently.

A variety of effective treatments are available for heroin addiction. Treatment tends to be more effective when heroin use is identified early. The treatments vary depending on the individual, but methadone, a synthetic opiate that blocks the effects of heroin and eliminates withdrawal symptoms, has a proven record of success for people addicted to heroin. Other pharmaceutical approaches, like LAAM (levo-alpha-acetyl-methadol), and many behavioral therapies also are used for treating heroin addiction. The following description of some of the most common approaches for treating heroin addiction come directly from NIDA's [National Institute on Drug Abuse] Research Report Series on heroin use.

Reprinted from Join Together, "Heroin Use: What Communities Should Know," 1999. An online article found at www.jointogether.org. Reprinted with permission.

The primary objective of detoxification is to relieve withdrawal symptoms while patients adjust to a drug-free state. Not in itself a treatment for addiction, detoxification is a useful step only when it leads into long-term treatment that is either drug-free (residential or outpatient) or uses medications as part of the treatment. The best documented drug-free treatments are the therapeutic community residential programs lasting at least 3 to 6 months.

Drug treatments for heroin addiction

Methadone treatment has been used effectively and safely to treat opioid addiction for more than 30 years. The programs use methadone as a substitute for heroin. Properly prescribed, methadone is not intoxicating or sedating, and its effects do not interfere with ordinary activities such as driving a car. The medication is taken orally and it suppresses narcotic withdrawal for 24 to 36 hours. Patients are able to perceive pain and have emotional reactions. Most important, methadone relieves the craving associated with heroin addiction; craving is a major reason for relapse. Among methadone patients, it has been found that normal street doses of heroin are ineffective at producing euphoria, thus making the use of heroin more easily extinguishable.

Methadone's effects last for about 24 hours—four to six times as long as those of heroin—so people in treatment need to take it only once a day. Also, methadone is medically safe even when used continuously for 10 years or more. Combined with behavioral therapies or counseling and other supportive services, methadone enables patients to stop using heroin (and other opiates) and return to more stable and productive lives.

LAAM, like methadone, is a synthetic opiate that can be used to treat heroin addiction. LAAM can block the effects of heroin for up to 72 hours with minimal side effects when taken orally. In 1993 the Food and Drug Administration approved the use of LAAM for treating patients addicted to heroin. Its long duration of action permits dosing just three times per week, thereby eliminating the need for daily dosing and take-home doses for weekends. LAAM will be increasingly available in clinics that already dispense methadone.

Naloxone and Naltrexone are medications that also block the effects of morphine, heroin, and other opiates. As antagonists, a drug that counteracts another drug, they are especially useful as antidotes. Naltrexone has long-lasting effects, ranging from 1 to 3 days, depending on the dose. Naltrexone blocks the pleasurable effects of heroin and is useful in treating some highly motivated individuals. Naltrexone has also been found to be successful in preventing relapse by former opiate addicts released from prison on probation.

Nondrug therapies for heroin addiction

Although behavioral and pharmacologic treatments can be extremely useful when employed alone, science has taught us that integrating both types of treatments will ultimately be the most effective approach. There are many effective behavioral treatments available for heroin addiction. These can include residential and outpatient approaches. An important task is to match the best treatment approach to meet the particular needs of the patient. Moreover, several new behavioral therapies, such as contingency management therapy and cognitive-behavioral interventions, show particular promise as treatments for heroin addiction. Contingency management therapy uses a voucher-based system, where patients earn "points" based on negative drug tests, which they can exchange for items that encourage healthy living. Cognitive-behavioral interventions are designed to help modify the patient's thinking, expectancies, and behaviors and to increase skills in coping with various life stressors. Both behavioral and pharmacological treatments help to restore a degree of normalcy to brain function and behavior.

It is important to note that most communities need an array of treatment methods to meet the needs of addicts, especially since most addicts abuse more than one drug, as well as alcohol, at the same time.

Some people believe that methadone and other pharmaceuticals just substitute one drug for another.

It is also necessary to mention that there are a lot of disagreements about the various treatment methods that exist. For instance, there are often controversies among treatment providers about the "best" modes of treatment. These disputes are sometimes rooted in philosophical differences about treatment. Some people believe that methadone and other pharmaceuticals just substitute one drug for another. Sometimes conflicts emerge as the result of competitive resources or funds from public and managed care programs. In other cases, there may be controversy about siting programs in residential parts of town.

Community leaders who are trying to expand treatment in their city or town must take the time to get to the roots of these and other controversies, so that they can be successful in overcoming them and ensuring help is available for all who need it.

8

Needle-Exchange Programs for Heroin Users Save Lives

Jon Fuller

Jon Fuller is an assistant director of the Adult Clinical AIDS Program at Boston Medical Center. Fuller was also the 1997–98 Margaret Pyne Professor of Theology at the Weston Jesuit School of Theology in Cambridge, Massachusetts.

The Catholic Church should support needle-exchange programs which supply heroin addicts with clean needles in exchange for used ones. International experience and research conducted in the United States confirm that needle-exchange programs (NEP's) help reduce the transmission of the HIV virus which causes AIDS. Supporting NEP's is morally right because the programs do not promote illicit activity and they save lives. The Catholic Church, therefore, has a moral duty to support the exchange programs in order to help protect the health and welfare of society's most vulnerable people.

In a remarkable rejection of scientific data and its own experts' opinions, the Clinton Administration announced in April 1998 its long-awaited decision regarding the expiring ban on Federal support of needle-exchange programs (N.E.P.'s).

The Administration's logic was not immediately obvious. While it recognized that N.E.P.'s reduce H.I.V. transmission and do not increase drug use, it refused to lift the ban but encouraged local governments to use their own resources to fund exchange programs. Since the Administration's stated reason was its concern that lifting the ban might send the wrong message to children, it is not evident why the states are being encouraged to do what the Federal Government should not.

In his reaction to the decision, R. Scott Hitt, an AIDS physician and chairman of the President's Advisory Council on H.I.V.-AIDS, was quoted in *The New York Times* as saying that "at best this is hypocrisy, at worst, it's a lie. And no matter what, it's immoral."

Reprinted from Jon Fuller, "Needle-Exchanging: Saving Lives," *America*, July 18–25, 1998.

As a church we need to consider carefully Dr. Hitt's evaluation, for it reminds us that a fundamental moral issue is at stake: the failure to act to save human lives. Dr. Hitt's criticism can as appropriately be directed toward the churches as toward the Administration: We can seem to be more concerned about potential "scandal" (sending the wrong message about drug use) than with N.E.P.'s ability to prevent lethal H.I.V. transmissions to particularly vulnerable populations.

Our silence or negative attitudes toward N.E.P.'s are puzzling, since the Catholic tradition is particularly well suited for responding to complicated questions such as needle exchange. We have nuanced tools for judging complex moral cases, we have a long tradition of engagement with the forces of society that particularly impinge on the poor and marginated, and we are in a unique position to provide moral leadership on this complex public issue that so confuses and frightens people.

Here I will review briefly the history and merits of needle-exchange programs from a public health perspective, and then demonstrate how, using traditional Catholic moral principles, we may not only tolerate but may even cooperate with these programs. Our particular responsibility to protect the lives of those without voice or power, those trapped in the cycle of addiction and those at risk for being infected should urge us to take a leadership role in the development of public policy on this life-threatening issue.

International experience

Based on the assessment that it is impossible to eliminate completely intravenous drug use in society, needle exchanges were first instituted in Amsterdam in 1983 to prevent the transmission of hepatitis B and H.I.V. (human immunodeficiency virus, the causative agent of AIDS), which can occur when needles are shared. While recovery from addiction was still sought as a long-term goal, N.E.P.'s were designed to protect addicts from these viruses in the meantime, and also to prevent secondary transmission to sexual partners and—in the case of pregnant women—transmission to developing infants. Needle exchanges have since been credited with a decrease in the number of new H.I.V. infections occurring among drug users in many cities around the globe. Indeed, three Catholic agencies sponsor needle exchanges in Australia. According to David Waterford of the Adelaide Diocesan AIDS Council, Southern Australia (with 55 exchange programs for a population of 1.2 million) has reported no new H.I.V. infections resulting from needle sharing over the period between 1995 and 1998.

The U.S. experience

In striking contrast to the decline in H.I.V. infections among addicts in these other countries, the United States has seen injection drug use increase as the source of H.I.V. infection among new AIDS cases from approximately 1 percent in 1981 to 31 percent of cases documented in 1997. When transmission from injectors to sexual partners and to infants is also included, 40 percent of new cases may be attributed to drug use. Three–fourths of H.I.V. transmissions to women and children have come from drug injectors, and among injectors who have been diagnosed with AIDS, 77 percent of women and 79 percent of men have come from communities of color.

Because of this increasing threat posed by needle transmissions, more than 100 needle exchanges have now been established in the United States. Many were begun as "guerilla" activities by addicts in recovery who understood the realities of addiction and the potential harm of needle sharing.

The human contact and protection from disease that [needle-exchange] programs offer communicates a powerful message to addicts that their lives and well-being are still valued.

However, as opposed to their fairly widespread acceptance in many other countries, needle-exchange programs encountered considerable resistance in the United States when they were first proposed. Neighborhoods voiced concerns about property values, security and the possibility that discarded needles might be left where children could play with them. Some objected that bringing needles into minority neighborhoods was a genocidal act, demonstrating an indifference to the particularly heavy burden of addiction already being borne by these communities. Despite a 1991 U.S. Government Accounting Office study that concluded that needle-exchange programs "hold some promise as an AIDS prevention strategy," Congress passed legislation in 1992 prohibiting the use of Federal funds to support needle-exchange programs until the Surgeon General could certify that they did not encourage drug use and were effective in reducing the spread of H.I.V.

The vast majority of U.S. N.E.P.'s are designed to be needle exchange, not needle distribution services—providing a clean needle and syringe only in exchange for a used set. In contrast with vending machines that dispense syringes in some European cities, U.S. programs consider human contact a critical aspect of the exchange, with education and referrals to health care and recovery programs being offered at every encounter. The human contact and protection from disease that these programs offer communicates a powerful message to addicts that their lives and well-being are still valued by the community, even though they may not yet be able to break the cycle of addictive behavior.

The U.S. Catholic response

In their 1989 pastoral letter on the AIDS epidemic, "Called to Compassion and Responsibility," the U.S. bishops raised serious concerns about needle-exchange programs as a means of limiting the spread of H.I.V. The bishops questioned whether these programs might increase drug use instead of reducing H.I.V. transmission and whether supporting them might send the wrong message by appearing to condone or even to make drug use easier. Although significant scientific literature has developed in support of exchange programs since that letter was written, there has been little further public discussion of needle exchange within the church, and almost no attention has been given to this issue in the ethical and theological literature. Several state bishops' conferences have spoken against exchange programs, but to my knowledge the only U.S. Catholic agency that has actively promoted N.E.P.'s is the Catholic Family Center in the Diocese of Rochester, N.Y.

Scientific evaluation of exchange programs

Numerous studies of the risks and benefits of needle exchange have now been published, and in 1995 an advisory panel of the National Research Council and the Institute of Medicine was constituted to review the state of the question. The group observed that, although existing drug paraphernalia laws were intended to decrease drug use, by inhibiting users from possessing needles "they unwittingly contribute to the sharing of contaminated ones. . . . While the act of giving a needle to an injection drug user has a powerful symbolism that has sparked fears about the potential negative effects of needle-exchange programs . . . there is no credible evidence that drug use is increased among participants or that it increases the number of new initiates to injection drug use."

After observing that public support for these programs tends to increase over time, the panel concluded that "well-implemented needle-exchange programs can be effective in preventing the spread of H.I.V. and do not increase the use of illegal drugs. We therefore recommend that the Surgeon General make the determination . . . necessary to rescind the present prohibition against applying any Federal funds to support needle exchange programs."

In February 1997 a consensus panel of the National Institutes of Health indicated that these programs "show reduction in risk behavior as high as 80 percent in injecting drug users, with estimates of a 30 percent reduction of H.I.V." The panel therefore "strongly recommended the lifting of government restrictions on needle-exchange programs and the legalization of pharmacy sales of sterile injecting equipment."

In March of 1998, the President's AIDS Council also urged that the ban be lifted, noting that every day 33 Americans are infected from dirty needles. Other endorsements of needle exchange have come from numerous groups concerned with the common good and the public health, including the American Medical Association, the American Public Health Association, the American Bar Association and the National Conference of Mayors. As increasing dialogue has occurred between operators of needle exchanges and public health and law enforcement agencies, some previously illegal operations have now become officially sponsored or at least tolerated.

Moral evaluation of exchange programs

While the consensus of scientific and public health opinion supports needle exchanges as providing significant benefits without causing harm, how do we analyze these programs from a moral perspective? Some judge that we must oppose them lest we be seen as condoning behavior judged to be gravely wrong, while others propose that we tolerate them by not opposing their being conducted by others. A third perspective, which can be justified by traditional moral principles, holds that the potential harm of needle sharing is so great that our commitment to the preservation of life and to caring for the most vulnerable members of society urges us to take the lead in supporting these programs.

Our tradition has long recognized that in a complex world we are frequently faced with the prospect of cooperating to some degree with individuals or groups whose goals we may not fully share. The "principle of cooperation" assists us in adjudicating a wide variety of questions, ranging from paying taxes to a government whose activities are not always condoned, to cooperating in an indirect manner with an illicit medical procedure. Although an extensive analysis of the principle and its application is not possible here, for the sake of discussion I propose to describe briefly how cooperation with N.E.P.'s can satisfy the principle's six criteria. (At the risk of employing a few unfamiliar phrases, the technical language traditionally used when invoking the principle has been included in this discussion.)

Advocacy on behalf of needle-exchange programs is consistent with an ethics of mercy, with [the Catholic Church's] traditional moral principles and with [the church's] mission to help the poor.

The first requirement—that the object of our action be good or morally neutral—is satisfied by the fact that simply exchanging a dirty needle for a sterile one is itself morally indifferent.

In the second test we must consider if our cooperation would be intending or promoting illicit activity. Since N.E.P.'s do not encourage or condone drug use—but only attempt to make drug use less harmful—our cooperation would be material and therefore permitted, whereas formal cooperation (explicit support or encouragement of drug use) would not.

The third criterion requires that the illicit activity (in this case, injection of a drug) not be the same as the action in which we are cooperating (exchange of needles). In the principle's technical language, cooperation with needle exchange would be judged as mediate (permitted) rather than immediate (forbidden).

In the fourth test our action must be distanced from the illicit act as much as possible. Since we would be cooperating with needle exchange rather than with drug injection, N.E.P.'s meet the test that our cooperation be remote, not proximate.

The fifth criterion—that cooperation be justified by a sufficiently grave reason—is self-evident in the lethal nature of H.I.V. transmission.

Finally, our assistance must not be necessary for the illicit action to be carried out. Since exchange programs provide no means for injection that a drug user does not already have, N.E.P.'s meet the requirement that our cooperation be dispensable, not indispensable.

This analysis suggests that permitting or even cooperating with N.E.P.'s would be allowed by traditional criteria, and that prudential judgment will be needed in each circumstance to determine the appropriate response of the local church. While toleration and cooperation can both be justified, I would propose that advocacy on behalf of N.E.P.'s is consistent with an ethics of mercy, with our traditional moral principles and with our pastoral mission to help the poor and marginalized. This approach recognizes that addiction is a disease whose natural history includes relapse, and it assists addicts in taking whatever small steps toward recovery are possible while protecting them and society from serious harm.

Central moral facts

I have asked many of my patients who became H.I.V.-infected through needle sharing how they regard exchange programs. While a few have been opposed—out of concern that they could send a mixed message—most wished that someone had cared enough for their welfare to make such an option available when they were in the throes of addiction, possibly preventing the life-threatening condition with which they now struggle.

I urge that we move beyond an understandable concern about sending mixed messages, to recognizing the central moral facts of the case. While neither condoning nor increasing drug use, N.E.P.'s save lives and bring addicts into treatment. A University of California study has calculated that up to 10,000 lives might have been saved thus far if we, as a nation, had supported needle exchange early on. It further estimated that "if current U.S. policies are not changed . . . an additional 5,150-11,329 preventable H.I.V. infections could occur by the year 2000." Our mandate to provide special attention to the health and welfare needs of the most vulnerable must certainly include injection drug users and their children and sexual partners. Let us engage our considerable resources in examining and discussing this question, exploring how best to support recovery from addiction while protecting vulnerable lives from life-threatening disease.

9

Needle-Exchange Programs Encourage Heroin Abuse

Joe Loconte

Joe Loconte is the deputy editor of Policy Review: The Journal of American Citizenship.

Scientific research does not support the claim that needle-exchange programs (NEPs) reduce the transmission of the HIV virus that causes AIDS. There are many reasons why needle-exchange programs—programs that provide heroin addicts clean needles in exchange for used ones—are ineffective. First, heroin addicts are not concerned about their health and therefore continue to exchange dirty needles with one another even when enrolled in NEPs and engage in risky sexual behavior that puts them at risk of contracting AIDS. Second, NEPs do not require addicts to enter treatment programs, and since addicts do not seek treatment voluntarily but only when forced to by the criminal justice system, they continue to abuse heroin while enrolled in NEPs. Finally, NEPs do not provide spiritual guidance about the addict's moral responsibility to quit, which gives the user free license to abuse drugs indefinitely.

In a midrise office building on Manhattan's West 37th Street, about two blocks south of the Port Authority bus terminal, sits the Positive Health Project, one of 11 needle-exchange outlets in New York City. This particular neighborhood, dotted by X-rated video stores, peep shows, and a grimy hot dog stand, could probably tolerate some positive health. But it's not clear that's what the program's patrons are getting.

The clients are intravenous (IV) drug users. They swap their used needles for clean ones and, it is hoped, avoid the AIDS virus, at least until their next visit. There's no charge, no hassles, no meddlesome questions. That's just the way Walter, a veteran heroin user, likes it.

"Just put me on an island and don't mess with me," he says, lighting up a cigarette.

Reprinted from Joe Loconte, "Killing Them Softly," *Policy Review*, August 1998. Reprinted with permission from *Policy Review*.

A tall, thinnish man, Walter seems weary for his 40-some years. Like many of the estimated 250,000 IV drug users in this city, he has spent years shooting up and has bounced in and out of detoxification programs. "Don't get the idea in your mind you're going to control it," he says. "I thought I could control it. But dope's a different thing. You just want it." Can he imagine his life without drugs? "I'm past that," he says, his face tightening. "The only good thing I do is getting high."

Heroin first, then breathing

Supporters of needle-exchange programs (NEPs), from AIDS activists to Secretary of Health and Human Services Donna Shalala, seem to have reached the same verdict on Walter's life. They take his drug addiction as a given, but want to keep him free of HIV by making sure he isn't borrowing dirty syringes. Says Shalala, "This is another life-saving intervention." That message is gaining currency, thanks in part to at least 112 programs in 29 states, distributing millions of syringes each year.

Critics say free needles just make it easier for addicts to go about their business: abusing drugs. Ronn Constable, a Brooklynite who used heroin and cocaine for nearly 20 years, says he would have welcomed the needle-exchange program—for saving him money. "An addict doesn't want to spend a dollar on anything else but his drugs," he says.

Do needle exchanges, then, save lives or fuel addiction?

The issue flared up earlier this year when Shalala indicated the Clinton administration would lift the ban on federal funding. Barry McCaffrey, the national drug policy chief, denounced the move, saying it would sanction drug use. Fearing a political debacle, the White House upheld the federal ban but continues to trumpet the effectiveness of NEPs. Meanwhile, Representative Gerald Solomon and Senator Paul Coverdell are pushing legislation in Congress to extend the prohibition indefinitely.

> *NEP advocates seem steeped in denial about the behavioral roots of the crisis, conduct left unchallenged by easy access to clean syringes.*

There is more than politics at work here. The debate reveals a deepening philosophical rift between the medical and moral approaches to coping with social ills.

Joined by much of the scientific community, the Clinton administration has tacitly embraced a profoundly misguided notion: that we must not confront drug abusers on moral or religious grounds. Instead, we should use medical interventions to minimize the harm their behavior invites. Directors of needle-exchange outlets pride themselves on running "nonjudgmental" programs. While insisting they do not encourage illegal drug use, suppliers distribute "safe crack kits" explaining the best ways to inject crack cocaine. Willie Easterlins, an outreach worker at a needle-stocked van in Brooklyn, sums up the philosophy this way: "I have to give you a needle. I can't judge," he says. "That's the first thing they teach us."

This approach, however well intentioned, ignores the soul-controlling darkness of addiction and the moral freefall that sustains it. "When addicts talk about enslavement, they're not exaggerating," says Terry Horton, the medical director of Phoenix House, one of the nation's largest residential treatment centers. "It is their first and foremost priority. Heroin first, then breathing, then food."

It is true that needle-sharing among IV drug users is a major source of HIV transmission, and that the incidence of HIV is rising most rapidly among this group—a population of more than a million people. Last year, about 30 percent of all new HIV infections were linked to IV drug use. The Clinton administration is correct to call this a major public-health risk.

Nevertheless, NEP advocates seem steeped in denial about the behavioral roots of the crisis, conduct left unchallenged by easy access to clean syringes. Most IV drug users, in fact, die not from HIV-tainted needles but from other health problems, overdoses, or homicide. By evading issues of personal responsibility, the White House and its NEP allies are neglecting the most effective help for drug abusers: enrollment in tough-minded treatment programs enforced by drug courts. Moreover, in the name of "saving lives," they seem prepared to surrender countless addicts to life on the margins—an existence of scheming, scamming, disease, and premature death.

Curious science

Over the last decade, NEPs have secured funding from local departments of public health to establish outlets in 71 cities. But that may be as far as their political argument will take them: Federal law prohibits federal money from flowing to the programs until it can be proved they prevent AIDS without encouraging drug use.

It's no surprise, then, that advocates are trying to enlist science as an ally. They claim that numerous studies of NEPs prove they are effective. Says Sandra Thurman, the director of the Office of National AIDS Policy, "There is very little doubt that these programs reduce HIV transmission." In arguing for federal funding, a White House panel on AIDS recently cited "clear scientific evidence of the efficacy of such programs."

The studies, though suggestive, prove no such thing. Activists tout the results of a New Haven study, published in the *American Journal of Medicine,* saying the program reduces HIV among participants by a third. Not exactly. Researchers tested needles from anonymous users—not the addicts themselves—to see if they contained HIV. They never measured "seroconversion rates," the portion of participants who became HIV positive during the study. Even Peter Lurie, a University of Michigan researcher and avid NEP advocate, admits that "the validity of testing of syringes is limited." A likely explanation for the decreased presence of HIV in syringes, according to scientists, is sampling error.

Another significant report was published in 1993 by the University of California and funded by the U.S. Centers for Disease Control. A panel reviewed 21 studies on the impact of NEPs on HIV infection rates. But the best the authors could say for the programs was that none showed a higher prevalence of HIV among program clients.

Even those results don't mean much. Panel members rated the scientific quality of the studies on a five-point scale: one meant "not valid," three "acceptable," and five "excellent." Only two of the studies earned ratings of three or higher. Of those, neither showed a reduction in HIV levels. No wonder the authors concluded that the data simply do not, and for methodological reasons probably cannot, provide clear evidence that needle exchanges decrease HIV infection rates.

The missing link

The most extensive review of needle-exchange studies was commissioned in 1993 by the U.S. Department of Health and Human Services (HHS), which directed the National Academy of Sciences (NAS) to oversee the project. Their report, "Preventing HIV Transmission: The Role of Sterile Needles and Bleach," was issued in 1995 and set off a political firestorm.

"Well-implemented needle-exchange programs can be effective in preventing the spread of HIV and do not increase the use of illegal drugs," a 15-member panel concluded. It recommended lifting the ban on federal funding for NEPs, along with laws against possession of injection paraphernalia. The NAS report has emerged as the bible for true believers of needle exchange.

It is not likely to stand the test of time. A truly scientific trial testing the ability of NEPs to reduce needle-sharing and HIV transmission would set up two similar, randomly selected populations of drug users. One group would be given access to free needles, the other would not. Researchers would follow them for at least a year, taking periodic blood tests.

None of the studies reviewed by NAS researchers, however, were designed in this way. Their methodological problems are legion: Sample sizes are often too small to be statistically meaningful. Participants are self-selected, so that the more health-conscious could be skewing the results. As many as 60 percent of study participants drop out. And researchers rely on self-reporting, a notoriously untrustworthy tool.

"Nobody has done the basic science yet," says David Murray, the research director of the Statistical Assessment Service, a watchdog group in Washington, D.C. "If this were the FDA applying the standard for a new drug, they would [block] it right there."

[A 1997 Montreal study] showed that addicts who used needle exchanges were more than twice as likely to become infected with HIV as those who didn't.

The NAS panel admitted its conclusions were not based on reviews of well-designed trials. Such studies, the authors agreed, simply do not exist. Not to worry, they said: "The limitations of individual studies do not necessarily preclude us from being able to reach scientifically valid conclusions." When all of the studies are considered together, they argued, the results are compelling.

"That's like tossing a bunch of broken Christmas ornaments in a box and claiming you have something nice and new and usable," Murray says. "What you have is a lot of broken ornaments." Two of the three physicians on the NAS panel, Lawrence Brown and Herbert Kleber, agree. They deny their report established anything like a scientific link between lower HIV rates and needle exchanges. "The existing data is flawed," says Kleber, executive vice president for medical research at Columbia University. "NEPs may, in theory, be effective, but the data doesn't prove that they are."

Some needle-exchange advocates acknowledge the dearth of hard science. Don Des Jarlais, a researcher at New York's Beth Israel Medical Center, writes in a 1996 report that "there has been no direct evidence that participation is associated with a lower risk" of HIV infection. Lurie, writing in the *American Journal of Epidemiology,* says that "no one study, on its own, should be used to declare the programs effective." Nevertheless, supporters insist, the "pattern of evidence" is sufficient to march ahead with the programs.

Mixed results

That argument might make sense if all the best studies created a happy, coherent picture. They don't. In fact, more-recent and better-controlled studies cast serious doubt on the ability of NEPs to reduce HIV infection.

In 1996, Vancouver researchers followed 1,006 intravenous cocaine and heroin users who visited needle exchanges, conducting periodic blood tests and interviews. The results, published in the British research journal *AIDS,* were not encouraging: About 40 percent of the test group reported borrowing a used needle in the preceding six months. Worse, after only eight months, 18.6 percent of those initially HIV negative became infected with the virus.

Dr. Steffanie Strathdee, of the British Columbia Centre for Excellence in HIV/AIDS, was the report's lead researcher. She found it "particularly disturbing" that needle-sharing among program participants, despite access to clean syringes, is common. Though an NEP advocate, Strathdee concedes that the high HIV rates are "alarming." Shepherd Smith, founder of Americans for a Sound AIDS/HIV Policy, says that compared to similar drug-using populations in the United States, the Vancouver results are "disastrous."

Though it boasts the largest needle-exchange program in North America, Vancouver is straining under an AIDS epidemic. When its NEP began in 1988, HIV prevalence among IV drug users was less than 2 percent. Today it's about 23 percent, despite a citywide program that dispenses 2.5 million needles a year.

A 1997 Montreal study is even more troubling. It showed that addicts who used needle exchanges were more than twice as likely to become infected with HIV as those who didn't. Published in the *American Journal of Epidemiology,* the report found that 33 percent of NEP users and 13 percent of nonusers became infected during the study period. Moreover, about three out of four program clients continued to share needles, roughly the same rate as nonparticipants.

The results are hard to dismiss. The report, though it did not rely on truly random selection, is the most sophisticated attempt so far to overcome the weaknesses of previous NEP studies. Researchers worked with a statistically significant sample (about 1,500), established test groups with better controls and lower dropout rates, and took greater care to account for "confounding variables." They followed each participant for an average of 21 months, taking blood samples every six months.

Blood samples don't lie. Attending an NEP was "a strong predictor" of the risk of contracting HIV, according to Julie Bruneau of the University of Montreal, the lead researcher. Bruneau's team then issued a warning: "We believe caution is warranted before accepting NEPs as uniformly beneficial in any setting."

The findings have sent supporters into a frenzy, with many fretting about their impact on public funding. "While it was important that the study be published," Peter Lurie complained to one magazine, "whether that information outweighs the political costs is another matter." In a bizarre *New York Times* op-ed, Bruneau recently disavowed some of her own conclusions. She said the results could be explained by higher-risk behavior engaged in by program users, a claim anticipated and rejected by her own report.

And that objection lands NEP supporters on the horns of a dilemma: Any control weaknesses in the Canadian reports are also present in the proexchange studies. "You can't have it both ways," Kleber says. "You can't explain away Montreal and Vancouver without applying the same scientific measures to the studies you feel are on your side."

Defending an expansion of the programs, AIDS policy czar Thurman says, "We need to let science drive the issue of needle exchange." The best that can be said for the evidence so far is that it doesn't tell us much. Without better-controlled studies, science cannot be hauled out as a witness for either side of the debate.

Death-defying logic

Critics of needle exchanges are forced to admit there's a certain logic to the concept, at least in theory: Give enough clean needles to an IV drug user and he won't bum contaminated "spikes" when he wants a fix.

But ex-addicts themselves, and the medical specialists who treat them, say it isn't that simple. "People think that everybody in shooting galleries worries about AIDS or syphilis or crack-addicted babies. That's the least of people's worries," says Jean Scott, the director of adult programs at Phoenix House in Manhattan. "While they're using, all they can think about is continuing to use and where they're going to get their next high."

Indeed, the NEP crowd mistakenly assumes that most addicts worry about getting AIDS. Most probably don't: The psychology and physiology of addiction usually do not allow them the luxury. "Once they start pumping their system with drugs, judgment disappears. Memory disappears. Nutrition disappears. The ability to evaluate their life needs disappears," says Eric Voth, the chairman of the International Drug Strategy Institute and one of the nation's leading addiction specialists. "What makes anybody think they'll make clean needles a priority?"

Ronn Constable, now a program director at Teen Challenge International in New York, says his addiction consumed him 24 hours a day, seven days a week. Addicts call it "chasing the bag": shooting up, feeling the high, and planning the next hit before withdrawal. "For severe addicts, that's all they do," Constable says. "Their whole life is just scheming to get their next dollar to get their next bundle of dope."

Ernesto Margaro fed his heroin habit for seven years, at times going through 40 bags—or $400—a day. He recalls walking up to a notorious drug den in the Bedford-Stuyvesant section of Brooklyn with a few of his friends. A man stumbled out onto the sidewalk and collapsed. They figured he was dying.

Margaro opened a fire hydrant on him. "When he finally came to, the first thing we asked him was where he got that dope from," he says. "We needed to know, because if it made him feel like that, we were going to take just a little bit less than he did."

This is typical of the hard-core user: The newest, most potent batch of heroin on the streets, the one causing the most deaths, is in greatest demand. "They run around trying to find out who the dead person copped from," says Scott, a drug-treatment specialist with 30 years' experience. "The more deaths you have, the more popular the heroin is. That's the mentality of the addict."

Needle entrepreneurs

Some younger addicts may at first be fearful of the AIDS virus, though that concern probably melts away as they continue to shoot up. But the hard-core abusers live in a state of deep denial. "I had them dying next to me," Constable says. "One of my closest buddies withered away. I never thought about it."

Needle-exchange programs are doing brisk business all over the country: San Diego, Seattle, Denver, Baltimore, Boston, and beyond. San Francisco alone hands out 2.2 million needles a year. If most addicts really aren't worried about HIV, then why do they come?

In most states, it is difficult to buy drug paraphernalia without a prescription. That makes it hard, some claim, to find syringes. But drug users can get them easily enough on the streets. The main reason they go to NEPs, it seems, is that the outlets are a free source of needles, cookers, cotton, and bleach. They're also convenient. They are run from storefronts or out of vans, and they operate several days a week at regular hours.

And they are hassle-free. Users are issued ID cards that entitle them to carry drug paraphernalia wherever they go. Police are asked to keep their distance lest they scare off clients.

Most programs require that users swap their old needles for new equipment, but people aren't denied if they "forget" to bring in the goods. And most are not rigid one-for-one exchanges. Jose Castellar works an NEP van at the corner of South Fifth Street and Marcy Avenue in Brooklyn. On a recent Thursday afternoon, a man walked up and mechanically dropped off 18 syringes in a lunch sack. Castellar recognized him as a regular, and gave him back 28—standard procedure. "It's sort of like an incentive," he explains.

It's the "incentive" part of the program that many critics find so objectionable. An apparently common strategy of NEP clients is to keep a handful of needles for themselves and sell the rest. Says Margaro, "They give you five needles. That's $2 a needle, that's $10. That's your next fix. That's all you're worried about."

It may also explain why many addicts who know they are HIV positive—older users such as Walter—still visit NEPs. Nobody knows how many there are, because no exchanges require blood tests. In New York, health officials say that perhaps half of the older IV addicts on the streets are infected.

Treatment communities that stress abstinence, responsibility, and moral renewal, backed up by tough law enforcement, are the best hope for addicts to escape drugs.

Defenders admit the system is probably being abused. "An addict is an addict. He's going to do what he needs to maintain his habit," says Easterlins, who works a van for ADAPT, one of New York City's largest needle-exchange programs. Naomi Fatt, ADAPT's executive director, is a little more coy. "We don't knowingly participate" in the black market for drug paraphernalia, she says. And if NEP clients are simply selling their syringes to other drug users? "We don't personally care how they get their sterile needles. If that's the only way they can save their lives is to get these needles on the streets, is that really so awful?"

Addiction and sex

In the debate over federal funding for NEPs, herein lies their siren song: Clean needles save lives. But there just isn't much evidence, scientific or otherwise, that free drug paraphernalia is protecting users.

The reason is drug addiction. Addicts attending NEPs continue to swap needles and engage in risky sexual behavior. All the studies that claim otherwise are based on self-reporting, an unreliable gauge.

By not talking much about drug abuse, NEP activists effectively sidestep the desperation created by addiction. When drug users run out of money for their habit, for example, they often turn to prostitution—no matter how many clean needles are in the cupboard. And the most common way of contracting HIV is, of course, sexual intercourse. "Sex is a currency in the drug world," says Horton of Phoenix House. "It is a major mode of HIV infection. And you don't address that with needle exchange."

At least a third of the women in treatment at the Brooklyn Teen Challenge had been lured into prostitution. About 15 percent of the female clients in Manhattan's Phoenix House contracted HIV by exchanging sex for drugs. In trying to explain the high HIV rates in Vancouver, researchers admitted "it may be that sexual transmission plays an important role."

Kleber, a psychiatrist and a leading addiction specialist, has been treating drug abusers for 30 years. He says NEPs, even those that offer education and health services, aren't likely to become beacons of behavior modification. "Addiction erodes your ability to change your behavior," he says. "And NEPs have no track record of changing risky sexual behavior."

Or discouraging other reckless choices, for that matter. James Curtis, the director of addiction services at the Harlem Hospital Center, says addicts are not careful about cleanliness and personal hygiene, so they often develop serious infections, such as septicemia, around injection areas. "It is false, misleading, and unethical," he says, "to give addicts the idea that they can be intravenous drug abusers without suffering serious self-injury."

A recent University of Pennsylvania study followed 415 IV drug users in Philadelphia over four years. Twenty-eight died during the study. Only five died from causes associated with HIV. Most died for other reasons: overdoses, homicide, heart disease, kidney failure, liver disease, and suicide. Writing in the *New England Journal of Medicine,* medical professors George Woody and David Metzger said that compared to the risk of HIV infection, the threat of death to drug abusers from other causes is "more imminent."

That proved tragically correct for John Watters and Brian Weil, two prominent founders of needle exchanges who died of apparent heroin overdoses. Indeed, deaths from drug dependence in cities with active needle programs have been on an upward trajectory for years. In New York City hospitals, the number has jumped from 413 in 1990 to 909 in 1996.

Pain creates change

Keeping drug users free of AIDS is a noble—but narrow—goal. Surely the best hope of keeping them alive is to get them off drugs and into treatment. Research from the National Institute for Drug Abuse (NIDA) shows that untreated opiate addicts die at a rate seven to eight times higher than similar patients in methadone-based treatment programs.

Needle suppliers claim they introduce addicts to rehab services, and Shalala wants local officials to include treatment referral in any new needle-exchange programs. But program staffers are not instructed to confront addicts about their drug habit. The assumption: Unless drug abusers are ready to quit on their own, it won't work.

This explains why NEP advocates smoothly assert they support drug treatment, yet gladly supply users with all the drug-injection equipment they need. "The idea that they will choose on their own when they're ready is nonsense," says Voth, who says he's treated perhaps 5,000 abusers of cocaine, heroin, and crack. "Judgment is one of the things that disappears with addiction. The worst addicts are the ones least likely to stumble into sobriety and treatment."

According to health officials, most addicts do not seek treatment voluntarily, but enter through the criminal-justice system. Even those who volunteer do so because of intense pressure from spouses or employers or raw physical pain from deteriorating health. In other words, they begin to confront some of the unpleasant consequences of their drug habit.

"The only way a drug addict is going to consider stopping is by experiencing pain," says Robert Dupont, a clinical professor of psychiatry at Georgetown University Medical School. "Pain is what helps to break their delusion," says David Batty, the director of Teen Challenge in Brooklyn. "The faster they realize they're on a dead-end street, the faster they see the need to change."

Justice for junkies

Better law enforcement, linked to drug courts and alternative sentencing for offenders, could be the best way to help them see the road signs up ahead. "It is common for an addict to say that jail saved his life," says Dr. Janet Lapey, the president of Drug Watch International. "Not until the drugs are out of his system does he usually think clearly enough to see the harm drugs are causing."

The key is to use the threat of jail time to prod offenders into long-term treatment. More judges seem ready to do so, and it's not hard to see why: In 1971, about 15 percent of all crime in New York was connected to drug use, according to law enforcement officials. In 1998, it's about 85 percent.

"There has been an enormous increase in drug-related crime because the only response of society has been a jail cell," says Brooklyn district attorney Charles Hynes. "But it is morally and fiscally irresponsible to warehouse nonviolent drug addicts." Since 1990, Hynes has helped reshape the city's drug-court system to offer nonviolent addicts a choice: two to four years in prison or a shot at rehabilitation and job training.

Many treatment specialists believe drug therapies will fail unless they're backed up with punishment and other pressures. Addicts need "socially imposed consequences" at the earliest possible stage—and the simplest way is through the criminal-justice system, says Dupont, a former director of NIDA. Sally Satel, a psychiatrist specializing in addiction, says "coercion can be the clinician's best friend."

That may not be true of all addicts, but it took stiff medicine to finally get the attention of Canzada Edmonds, a heroin user for 27 years. "I was in love with heroin. I took it into the bathroom, I took it into church," she says. "I was living in a fantasy. I was living in a world all to myself."

And she was living in Washington, D.C., which in the early 1990s had passed tougher sentencing laws for felony drug offenders. After her third felony arrest, a district judge said she faced a possible 30-year term in prison—or a trip to a residential rehab program. Edmonds went to Teen Challenge in New York in January 1995 and has been free of drugs ever since.

Reducing harm

Needle-exchange advocates chafe at the thought of coercing drug users into treatment. This signals perhaps their most grievous omission: They refuse to challenge the self-absorption that nourishes drug addiction.

In medical terms, it's called "harm reduction"—accept the irresponsible behavior and try to minimize its effects with health services and education. Some needle exchanges, for example, distribute guides to safer drug use. A pamphlet from an NEP in Bridgeport, Connecticut, explains how to prepare crack cocaine for injection. It then urges users to "take care of your veins. Rotate injection sites. . . ."

"Harm reduction is the policy manifestation of the addict's personal wish," says Satel, "which is to use drugs without consequences." The concept is backed by numerous medical and scientific groups, including the American Medical Association, the American Public Health Association, and the National Academy of Sciences.

In legal terms, harm reduction means the decriminalization of drug use. Legalization advocates, from financier George Soros to the Drug Policy Foundation, are staunch needle-exchange supporters. San Francisco mayor Willie Brown, who presides over perhaps the nation's busiest needle programs, is a leading voice in the harm-reduction chorus. "It is time," he has written, "to stop allowing moral or religious tradition to define our approach to a medical emergency."

It is time, rather, to stop medicalizing what is fundamentally a moral problem. Treatment communities that stress abstinence, responsibility, and moral renewal, backed up by tough law enforcement, are the best hope for addicts to escape drugs and adopt safer, healthier lifestyles.

Despite different approaches, therapeutic communities share at least one goal: drug-free living. Though they commonly regard addiction as a disease, they all insist that addicts take full responsibility for their cure. Program directors aren't afraid of confrontation, they push personal responsibility, and they tackle the underlying causes of drug abuse.

The Clinton administration already knows these approaches are working. NIDA recently completed a study of 10,000 drug abusers who entered nearly 100 different treatment programs in 11 cities. Researchers looked at daily drug use a year before and a year after treatment. Long-term residential settings—those with stringent anti-drug policies—did best: Heroin use dropped by 71 percent, cocaine use by 68 percent, and illegal activity in general by 62 percent.

NEP supporters are right to point out that these approaches are often expensive and cannot reach most of the nation's estimated 1.2 million IV drug users. Syringe exchanges, they say, are a cost-effective alternative.

NEPs may be cheaper to run, but they are no alternative; they offer no remedy for the ravages of drug addiction. The expense of long-term residential care surely cannot be greater than the social and economic costs of failing to liberate large populations from drug abuse.

Phoenix House, with residential sites in New York, New Jersey, California, and Texas, works with about 3,000 abusers a day. It is becoming a crucial player in New York City's drug courts, targeting roughly 500 adolescents and 1,400 adults. "Coerced treatment works better than noncoerced," says Anne Swern, a deputy district attorney in Brooklyn. "Judicially coerced residential treatment works best of all."

Nonviolent drug felons are diverted into the program as part of a parole agreement or as an alternative to prison. They sign up for a tightly scripted routine of counseling, education, and work, with rewards and sanctions to reinforce good behavior. Though clients are not locked in at night, police send out "warrant teams" to make regular visits.

Prosecutors and judges like the approach because of its relatively high retention rates. Sixty percent graduate from the program, Swern says, compared to the 13 percent national average for all drug programs. Graduates usually undergo 24 months of treatment and must find housing and employment. Says Horton, "The ability of a judge to tell an addict it's Rikers Island or Phoenix House is a very effective tool."

Narcotics Anonymous (NA), like Alcoholics Anonymous (AA), is a community-based association of recovering addicts. Since its formation in the 1950s, NA has stressed the therapeutic value of addicts helping other addicts; its trademark is the weekly group meeting, run out of homes, churches, and community centers.

"You get the benefit of hearing how others stayed clean today, with the things life gave them," says Tim, a 20–year heroin user and NA member since 1995. NA offers no professional therapists, no residential facilities, no clinics. Yet its 12-step philosophy, adapted from AA, is perhaps the most common treatment strategy in therapeutic communities.

The 12-step model includes admitting there is a problem, agreeing to be open about one's life, and making amends where harm has been done. The only requirement for NA membership is a desire to stop using. "Complete and continuous abstinence provides the best foundation for recovery and personal growth," according to NA literature.

As in AA, members must admit they cannot end their addiction on their own. The philosophy's second step is the belief that "a power greater than ourselves can restore us to sanity." NA considers itself nonreligious, but urges members to seek "spiritual awakening"—however they choose to define it—to help them stay clean.

Teen Challenge, founded in 1958 by Pentecostal minister David Wilkerson, is a pioneer in therapeutic communities and has achieved some remarkable results in getting addicts off drugs permanently. One federal study found that 86 percent of the program's graduates were drug free seven years after completing the regimen. On any given day, about 2,500 men and women are in its 125 residential centers nationwide.

The program uses an unapologetically Christian model of education and counseling. Moral and spiritual problems are assumed to lie at the root of drug addiction. Explains a former addict, who was gang-raped when she was 13, "I didn't want to feel what I was feeling about the rape—the anger, the hate—so I began to medicate. It was my way of coping." Though acknowledging that the reasons for drug use are complex, counselors make Christian conversion the linchpin of recovery. Ronn Constable says he tried several rehab programs, but failed to change his basic motivation until he turned to faith in Christ. He has been steadily employed and free of drugs for 11 years.

"Sin is the fuel behind addiction," Constable says, "but the Lord says He will not let me be tempted beyond what I can bear." He is typical of former addicts at Teen Challenge, who say their continued recovery hinges on their trust in God and obedience to the Bible. Warns Edmonds, "If you do not make a decision to turn your will and your life completely over to the power of God, then you're going to go right back." Or as C.S. Lewis wrote in another context, "The hardness of God is kinder than the softness of man, and His compulsion is our liberation."

Ill-conceived public policy

Whether secular or religious, therapeutic communities all emphasize the "community" part of their strategy. One reason is that addicts must make a clean break not only from their drug use, but from the circle of friends who help them sustain it. That means a 24-hour-a-day regimen of counseling, education, and employment, usually for 12 to 24 months, safely removed from the culture of addiction.

This is the antithesis of needle-exchange outlets, which easily become magnets for drug users and dealers. Nancy Sosman, a community activist in Manhattan, calls the Lower East Side Harm Reduction Center and Needle Exchange Program "a social club for junkies." Even supporters such as Bruneau warn that NEPs could instigate "new socialization" and "new sharing networks" among otherwise isolated drug users. Some, under the banner of AIDS education, hail this function of the programs. Allan Clear, the executive director of New York's Harm Reduction Coalition, told one magazine, "There needs to be a self-awareness of what an NEP supplies: a meeting place where networks can form."

Meanwhile, activists decry a lack of drug paraphernalia for eager clients. They call the decision to withhold federal funding "immoral." They want NEPs massively expanded, some demanding no limits on distribution. Says one spokesman, "The one-to-one rule in needle exchange isn't at all connected to reality." New York's ADAPT program gives out at least 350,000 needles a year. "But to meet the demand," says Fatt, "we'd need to give out a million a day."

A million a day? Now that would be a *Brave New World* (a novel by Aldous Huxley in which the government supplies its people with free drugs): Intravenous drug users with lots of drugs, all the needles they want, and police-free zones in which to network. Are we really to believe this strategy will contain the AIDS virus?

This is not compassion, it is ill-conceived public policy. This is not "saving lives," but abandoning them—consigning countless thousands to drug-induced death on the installment plan. For when a culture winks at drug use, it gets a population of Walters: "Don't get the idea in your mind you're going to control it."

10

Methadone Treatment Is a Practical Solution to Heroin Addiction

Stephen Chapman

Stephen Chapman is a columnist and editorial writer for the Chicago Tribune. *His twice-weekly column on national and international affairs appears in some sixty papers across the country.*

Methadone treatment is the solution to the growing heroin problem in the United States. Methadone—an opiate like heroin without heroin's destructive effect on the body—alleviates the withdrawal symptoms of people trying to stop using heroin. The excessive regulations on the drug should be relaxed so that more addicts can enter methadone treatment programs and begin leading healthy, productive lives.

Americans are endlessly searching for solutions to our drug problem. Beefing up law enforcement has cost a lot but accomplished little. Legalization is too scary. Education and "just say no" campaigns haven't gotten rid of the dealers or the addicts. Is there another answer?

It so happens there is, at least for the growing problem of heroin addiction, but it comes with a catch. This solution costs very little, reduces the crime and other social ills caused by drug use and doesn't involve legalization. What's the catch? The catch is that we have to be sensible for a change.

The remedy is methadone, which has been used for nearly 30 years to relieve the symptoms of withdrawal from heroin addiction. Drug experts widely agree that of all the forms of drug treatment we have tried, methadone is by far the most effective.

Junkies who turn to methadone, studies have shown, improve their lives in all sorts of ways. They commit less crime. They reduce or eliminate their use of illegal drugs. They are less apt to contract the virus that causes AIDS. They pose less of a danger to themselves and everyone else.

Reprinted from Stephen Chapman, "Resisting a Solution to the Drug Problem," *Conservative Chronicle*, August 12, 1998. Reprinted with permission from Creators Syndicate.

Many patients have to stay on the drug indefinitely, but this is no cause for concern. At about $4,000 a year to participate in a treatment program, it's much cheaper than a heroin habit, which can cost 10 times that much. In the right dose, methadone doesn't produce a "high" or a sedative effect. Patients remain clear-headed, alert and able to carry on normal daily tasks, from working to driving. There are no significant side effects or long-term risks.

The downside? There is none. Skeptics lament the diversion of some methadone to the black market and disapprove of trading one form of opiate addiction for another.

But this is petty carping. Methadone is never going to he a big party drug. The only people likely to buy it are addicts who would otherwise buy heroin—possibly people who want to quit but can't or won't go to a clinic. How, exactly, does that worsen the drug problem?

True, it makes absolutely no sense to trade one addiction for another —unless, of course, you want to help junkies become rational, productive, law-abiding citizens whose drug "problem" is no worse than that of a depressed person on Prozac. Why should it bother us if reformed heroin addicts need a legal drug to stay clean? Isn't staying clean enough of an accomplishment?

Junkies who turn to methadone, studies have shown, improve their lives in all sorts of ways.

Unfortunately, our national policy on methadone has been defined by its minor dangers, not its great promise.

Ethan Nadelmann and Jennifer McNeely of the Lindesmith Center, a drug-policy think tank in New York, wrote recently in *The Public Interest*, "Methadone-maintenance patients—many of whom stay in treatment for 20 or 30 years—are often subject to stricter supervision than convicted probationers and parolees."

An addict who wants methadone treatment has to go to a special clinic that is staffed by doctors who have been specifically authorized to dispense the drugs, laboring under a welter of regulations on staffing, security, record-keeping and treatment. In some places, an addict has to go to the clinic every day to get her medicine, even if it means hours of driving. Regular urine tests are mandatory.

As a result, methadone treatment costs far more than it needs to, and many addicts give it up or never start it because of the hassle. A study issued last year by the National Academy of Sciences found that current policy "puts too much emphasis on protecting society from methadone and not enough on protecting society from the epidemics of addiction, violence and infectious diseases that methadone can help reduce."

The best alternative is simple: Make methadone available by prescription, like other medicines, letting doctors dispense it to their patients who need it. Some addicts would continue to prefer clinics that provide counseling and job help. But, for the majority, whose only real need is methadone, the change would be a great boon.

Making methadone easier to get would almost certainly entice many heroin addicts to kick the habit. In Amsterdam, where methadone is much easier to get legally, the proportion of addicts in treatment is three times higher than in the United States.

Dr. Marc Shinderman, a psychiatrist who owns and runs the well-regarded Center for Addictive Problems in Chicago, argues that the medicine is now "severely over-regulated" and notes studies showing that addicts improve when they get no services but only methadone. "There would be some abuses with greater access, but they would be trivial compared to the benefits in terms of crime in the streets, illness and illicit drug use," he says.

Drug enforcers think we need even tighter controls. But they've got it backward. Methadone is a solution, not a problem. If we're not willing to embrace it, we should stop pretending that solutions are what we want.

11

Methadone Treatment Programs Create More Heroin Addicts

Theodore Dalrymple

Theodore Dalrymple is a columnist for the Sunday Telegraph, *a newspaper serving the United Kingdom.*

Methadone—an opiate like heroin—is frequently prescribed to heroin addicts to help them withdraw from the illegal drug. Methadone treatment provides a way for addicts to slowly withdraw from heroin use by substituting methadone—which has fewer serious side effects—for heroin. The treatment also helps prevent the use of dirty needles which are used to shoot heroin and can lead to the transmission of the virus that causes AIDS. In addition, because it is free, Methadone reduces the motives for committing crime to fuel heroin habits. Although some addicts do recover by using methadone as prescribed, many others take the free methadone from the clinics and sell it to other addicts in order to buy more heroin for themselves. Moreover, for every addict who stops using heroin, drug pushers will hook someone else on the drug who may resort to crime in the future. Those who dispense methadone endorse its use in order to protect their jobs.

A little boy aged two died in Solihull (in the United Kingdom) recently of poisoning by his mother's methadone, the drug that is prescribed to heroin addicts to "cure" them of their addiction.

There is nothing particularly unusual about a child poisoning itself with adult's medicine and there are many fatal substances to take besides methadone. Still, I can't help noticing that the number of deaths from methadone (both deliberate and accidental) is rising: in Manchester [England], it doubled in a single year.

Reprinted from Theodore Dalrymple, "Methadone in Their Madness," *Sunday Telegraph*, August 24, 1997. Reprinted with permission from the author.

63

The rationale for substituting methadone for heroin is complex. First, it establishes addicts on a regular, controlled regime of medication from which it may be possible slowly to withdraw them. Second, it prevents at least some of them from injecting themselves [with heroin], which is dangerous and, if needles are shared, can lead to infection with the AIDs virus. Third, because it is prescribed free, it reduces the motives for committing crimes. Research shows that heroin addicts commit fewer crimes once they are on methadone.

Nevertheless, methadone is no panacea, and I wonder whether it isn't part of the problem rather than a solution. Much methadone is diverted on to the black market, sales that fund the prescribed person's continued use of heroin and cause deaths among the non-addicted. And while the prescription of methadone may reduce the amount of crime committed by addicts, it doesn't stop it altogether: in the past 12 months 15 per cent of people prescribed methadone in Glasgow [Scotland] received a prison sentence, and a further 10 per cent were arrested at least once.

Moreover, it doesn't follow that because methadone prescription reduces the number of crimes committed by individual addicts that the number of crimes committed by addicts in society as a whole likewise falls: on the contrary. If an addict ceases to use heroin once he is prescribed methadone, it means that drug-pushers have a motive to hook someone else. What you end up with is at least the same amount of crime, but more addicts.

Much methadone is diverted on to the black market, sales that fund the prescribed person's continued use of heroin.

That is why, in a society awash with methadone, drug-motivated crime does not decline as it should if methadone were a solution to the problem. An increase in total crime in society is perfectly compatible with a reduction in crime by addicts prescribed methadone. And the people really addicted to methadone are not the people who take it, but the people who prescribe it. They are at least as dependent upon it for their livelihood as the late Pablo Escobar was upon cocaine for his.

The new professional drug-pushers have insinuated themselves everywhere. Like all good bureaucrats, they argue that the worse they make things, the more of them are needed. They claim to be the solution to the problem they create.

The British Medical Journal—by far the most politically correct publication in the country—has gone over to the side of the bureaucratic drug-pushers. It is even running something of a campaign at the moment to make methadone more widely available in prisons. A few weeks ago it ran an article suggesting that prisoners had a right to clean needles with which to inject themselves [with heroin] safely. If the *BMJ* had written the American *Declaration of Independence* it would, presumably, have held the following rights to be self-evident and unalienable: those to life, liberty, the pursuit of happiness and clean needles in prison.

However, the *BMJ* omits to mention that prisoners and drug addicts sometimes grossly exaggerate the severity of the withdrawal effects from heroin and methadone in order to obtain sympathy and, more importantly, prescriptions. (How many people know that withdrawal from alcohol drunk to excess for a long time is infinitely more distressing and dangerous than withdrawal from opiates? Oddly enough, this fact is not used to call for the dissemination *ad libitum* of whisky inside prison.)

Before long methadone-pushers will be in every prison. The more people who die of methadone poisoning, and the more who take methadone for the rest of their lives, the more such pushers we need. Every cloud has a silver lining—at public expense, of course.

12

Heroin Addicts Should Have Supervised Access to Heroin

Ethan Nadelmann

Ethan Nadelmann is the director of the Lindesmith Center, a drug-policy research institute.

Switzerland is experimenting with prescribing heroin to heroin addicts who have not been successful in quitting on their own. The Swiss experiment is based on the assumption that achieving a drug-free society is impossible, and therefore the best way to mitigate the social and economic costs of drug abuse is to assume a "harm reduction" approach. Such an approach—while still aggressively punishing drug dealers—works with drug users to reduce overdose, disease, and death. In addition to supplying controlled amounts of heroin to addicts each day, the Swiss government provides clean rooms where addicts can inject heroin. So far the experiment has shown that heroin causes little damage and that the addict's health improves if drug use is monitored. The United States should abandon its ineffective war on drugs—which punishes both dealers and users—and adopt a heroin prescription program.

The Swiss government is selling heroin to hard-core drug users. But in doing so the government isn't offhandedly facilitating drug abuse; it's conducting a national scientific experiment to determine whether prescribing heroin, morphine, and injectable methadone will save Switzerland both money and misery by reducing crime, disease, and death.

The Swiss deal with drug users much as the U.S. and other countries do—prisons, drug-free residential treatment programs, oral methadone, etc.—but they also know that these approaches are not enough. They first tried establishing a "Needle Park" in Zurich, an open drug scene where people could use drugs without being arrested. Most Zurichers, including the police, initially regarded the congregation of illicit drug injectors in one place as preferable to scattering them throughout the city. But the

Reprinted from Ethan Nadelmann, "Switzerland's Heroin Experiment," *National Review*, July 10, 1995, pp. 46–47. Copyright © 1995 National Review, Inc., 215 Lexington Avenue, New York, NY 10016. Reprinted by permission.

66

scene grew unmanageable, and city officials closed it down in February 1992. A second attempt faced similar problems and was shut down in March 1995.

So Needle Park wasn't the solution, but the heroin-prescription program might be. In it, 340 addicts receive a legal supply of heroin each day from one of the nine prescribing programs in eight different cities. In addition, 11 receive morphine, and 33 receive injectable methadone. The programs accept only "hard-core" junkies—people who have been injecting for years and who have attempted and failed to quit. Participants are not allowed to take the drug home with them. They have to inject on site and pay 15 francs (approximately $13) per day for their dose.

The idea of prescribing heroin to junkies in hopes of reducing both their criminal activity and their risk of spreading AIDS and other diseases took off in 1991. Expert scientific and ethical advisory bodies were established to consider the range of issues. The International Narcotics Control Board—a United Nations organization that oversees international antidrug treaties—had to be convinced that the Swiss innovation was an experiment, which is permitted under the treaty, rather than an official shift in policy. In Basel, opponents of the initiative demanded a city-wide referendum—in which 65 per cent of the electorate approved a local heroin-prescription program. The argument that swayed most people was remarkably straightforward: only a controlled scientific experiment could determine whether prescribing heroin to addicts is feasible and beneficial.

Heroin per se causes very few, if any, problems when it is used in a controlled fashion and administered in hygienic conditions.

The experiment started in January 1994. The various programs differ in some respects, although most provide supplemental doses of oral methadone, psychological counseling, and other assistance. Some are located in cities like Zurich, others in towns like Thun, which sits at the foot of the Bernese Alps. Some provide just one drug, while others offer a choice. Some allow clients to vary their dose each day, while others work with clients to establish a stable dosage level. One of the programs in Zurich is primarily for women. The other Zurich program permits addicts to take home heroin-injected cigarettes known as reefers, or "sugarettes," (since heroin is called "sugar" by Swiss junkies). It also conducted a parallel experiment in which 12 clients were prescribed cocaine reefers for up to 12 weeks. The results were mixed, with many of the participants finding the reefers unsatisfying. However, since more than two-thirds of Swiss junkies use cocaine as well as heroin, the Swiss hope to refine the cocaine experiment in the future.

The national experiment is designed to answer a host of questions that also bubble up in debates over drug policy in the United States, but that our drug-war blinders force us to ignore. Can junkies stabilize their drug use if they are assured of a legal, safe, and stable source of heroin? Can they hold down a job even if they're injecting heroin two or three times a day? Do they stop using illegal heroin and cut back on use of other illegal drugs? Do they commit fewer crimes? Are they healthier and less likely to contract the HIV virus? Are they less likely to overdose? Is it possible to overcome the "not in my back yard" objections that so often block methadone and other programs for addicts?

The answers to these questions are just beginning to come in. In late 1994, the Social Welfare Department in Zurich held a press conference to issue its preliminary findings: 1) Heroin prescription is feasible, and has produced no black market in diverted heroin. 2) The health of the addicts in the program has clearly improved. 3) Heroin prescription alone cannot solve the problems that led to the heroin addiction in the first place. 4) Heroin prescription is less a medical program than a social-psychological approach to a complex personal and social problem. 5) Heroin per se causes very few, if any, problems when it is used in a controlled fashion and administered in hygienic conditions.

Program administrators also found little support for the widespread belief that addicts' cravings for heroin are insatiable. When offered practically unlimited amounts of heroin (up to 300 milligrams three times a day), addicts soon realized that the maximum doses provided less of a "flash" than lower doses, and cut back their dosage levels accordingly.

On the basis of these initial findings, the Swiss federal government approved an expansion of the experiment—one that may offer an opportunity to address the bigger question that small-scale experiments and pilot projects cannot answer: Can the controlled prescription of heroin to addicts take the steam out of the illegal drug markets?

Switzerland's prescription experiment fits in with the two-track strategy Switzerland and other Western European countries have been pursuing since the mid-1980s: tough police measures against drug dealers, and a "harm reduction" approach toward users. The idea behind harm reduction is to stop pretending that a drug-free society is a realistic goal; focus first on curtailing the spread of AIDS—a disease that will have cost the U.S. $15.2 billion by the end of 1995, and the lives of over 125,000 Americans—and later on curtailing drug use.

> *The point of [heroin prescription] isn't to coddle drug users. It's to reduce the human and economic costs of drug use.*

The effort to make sterile syringes more available through needle-exchange programs and the sale of needles in pharmacies and vending machines epitomizes the harm-reduction philosophy. Swiss physicians and pharmacists—along with their professional associations—are outspoken in their support of these initiatives. Study after study, including one conducted for the U.S. Centers for Disease Control, show that increasing needle availability reduces the spread of AIDS, gets dirty syringes, off the streets, and saves money.

The Swiss have also created legal Fixerräume, or "injection rooms," where addicts can shoot up in a regulated, sanitary environment. Swiss public-health officials regard this harm-reduction innovation as preferable to the two most likely alternatives: open injection of illicit drugs in public places, which is distasteful and unsettling to most non-addicts; and the more discreet use of drugs in unsanctioned "shooting galleries" that are frequently dirty, violent, controlled by drug dealers, and conducive to needle sharing. Five Fixerräume are now open in Switzerland. Initial evaluations indicate that they are effective in reducing HIV transmission and the risk of overdose.

So what does the future hold? Last month, Switzerland's governing body, the Federal Council, voted to expand the number of prescription slots to 1,000: 800 for heroin, 100 each for morphine and injectable methadone. Interior minister Ruth Dreifuss, who initially was skeptical of the experiment, is now a strong supporter. She is backed by the ministers of justice, defense, and finance, who together constitute what has become known as "the drug delegation" of the Federal Council. The three leading political parties have combined to issue a joint report on drug policy that supports the heroin experiment and other harm-reduction initiatives. Outside Switzerland, the Dutch are about to embark on their own modest experiment with heroin prescription. The Australians, who recently conducted an extensive feasibility study, seem likely to start a heroin-prescription program. In Germany, officials in Frankfurt, Hamburg, Karlsruhe, Stuttgart, and elsewhere are seeking permission from the central government to begin their own heroin-prescription projects.

While these countries experiment with more sensible and humane approaches to drug policy, the United States clings to a war not only against drug dealers, but also against drug users. Most scientific researchers studying drug abuse acknowledge that the Swiss experiment makes sense socially, economically, and morally. The point of these innovations isn't to coddle drug users. It's to reduce the human and economic costs of drug use—costs paid not only by users but also by non-users through increased health-care, justice, and law-enforcement expenditures.

But no distinguished researcher seems prepared to take on all the forces blocking a heroin-prescription experiment in the United States. Through our reticence, we are shutting our eyes to drug policy options that could reduce crime, death, and disease and ultimately save this country billions of dollars.

13

Supplying Addicts with Heroin Is Unethical

Robert Maginnis

Robert Maginnis is a senior policy adviser with the Family Research Council. He visited five Swiss heroin clinics during the Swiss experiment of supplying addicts with heroin.

Baltimore is considering adopting a heroin maintenance program such as the one that Switzerland established during a two-year experiment in which the Swiss government provided addicts with heroin for a nominal fee. Heroin maintenance programs are based on the false belief that creating a drug-free society is impossible, and that "harm reduction"—reducing the negative effects of drug use, such as poor health and crime—is the only solution to the drug problem. The Swiss claim that maintenance programs improve the health of addicts, allow them to live normal lives, and reduce crime. But the Swiss experiment was flawed because it did not use a representative sample of heroin addicts and relied on the addicts themselves to report about their engagement in criminal activity. Furthermore, more addicts died in the program than became drug-free, and although some addicts found employment, the same number went on welfare. Heroin maintenance programs are unethical, because they keep the addict locked into a destructive and potentially fatal lifestyle.

European drug legalizers have long touted the merits of heroin giveaways. Now, those same people want to give heroin to addicts in Baltimore—where almost half of all adults arrested test positive for opiates. If Baltimore's "pilot" program is declared a "success," expect heroin giveaways to spread across America.

Heroin giveaways are an extension of the "harm reduction" philosophy that says drug use cannot be eliminated, so society should try to reduce the harm" it causes. The best known "harm reduction" programs are needle exchanges. Both programs pave the way for drug legalization, increased drug use, and the certain deaths of many addicts.

Reprinted from Robert Maginnis, "Treat Addicts with Drug Maintenance? Disputed Results," *The Washington Times*, August 16, 1998. Copyright © 1998 News World Communications, Inc. Reprinted with permission from *The Washington Times*.

The *Baltimore Sun* quoted that city's health commissioner, Dr. Peter Beilenson, who said, "It will be politically difficult, but I think it's going to happen." He claims heroin "maintenance"—a euphemism for giving pharmaceutical-grade heroin to addicts in an effort to improve their physical and social well-being—"would be carefully controlled by health care providers."

Dr. Beilenson's announcement comes on the heels of a June 6 New York City seminar promoting heroin for "medical" reasons. Billionaire George Soros, the nation's leading drug legalizer, was the primary event sponsor. A seminar attendee, David Vlahov, a professor at the Johns Hopkins School of Public Health in Baltimore, is involved in planning the nation's first heroin program.

Vlahov and Beilenson have Baltimore Mayor Kurt Schmoke's full support. Mr. Schmoke is a board member of the pro-legalization, Soros-sponsored Drug Policy Foundation. In May 1997, Mr. Schmoke urged President Bill Clinton at the National Mayors Conference to endorse heroin maintenance.

At the New York heroin seminar, Vlahov and Beilenson were impressed by Switzerland's recent three-year study. Mr. Vlahov said "heroin maintenance is an outreach strategy to bring people into the [treatment] system." Dr. Beilenson claims a U.S. version of the Swiss program would help most addicts become drug-free and reduce both crime and homelessness. The Swiss heroin experiment began in 1994. The project, which officially ended in December 1996, involved 1,146 addicts who paid nominal fees for up to three injections a day to determine whether giving heroin to addicts could "normalize" their lives.

In July 1997, the Swiss government labeled the experiment a "success."

The Swiss experiment was flawed

Some outsiders disagree with this assessment. The World Health Organization labeled the heroin trials as "quasi-experimental" and Dr. Oskar Schroeder, the then-president of the United Nations International Narcotics Control Board, called Switzerland's heroin experiment "a first step toward legalization."

The Swiss project was scientifically flawed. Neither the number of addicts nor the mix of participants receiving heroin, morphine or methadone was held constant. The initial goal of abstinence was abandoned in favor of a "better understanding of heroin addiction." Prison inmates and mental patients were added midway through the project.

Most of the new heroin "patients" (61 percent) were taken from methadone programs (a synthetic opiate that blocks the effects of heroin), and 19 percent weren't even heroin addicts before the Swiss government started drug dealing.

Thomas Zeltner, director of the Swiss Federal office of Public Health, participated in the New York heroin conference. He said heroin maintenance is part of a "holistic approach" to solving the drug problem.

Mr. Zeltner does not believe a drug-free society is possible, but admits heroin projects are not a panacea and "may not work for other nations." It's not clear heroin giveaways work for Switzerland. More Swiss addicts died while in the program than became drug-free. As for crime rates, police were not included in the experiment's design and operation, so reported crime decreases were exclusively based on self-reporting by addicts rather than law enforcement data.

"Harm reductionists" want to keep judgement-impaired addicts in their deadly lifestyle until they die or quit by chance.

Addicts' health improved not because they were given free dope, but because they were provided routine health care, food and housing. Addicts' employment did rise for menial public service jobs, but so did welfare dependency.

Baltimore's Dr. Beilenson was joined at the heroin conference by health researchers and officials from cities like Chicago, New Haven, San Antonio, and Sacramento. These officials are rightly concerned about the growing heroin scourge. Unfortunately, they embrace the Swiss model and are planning an American heroin pilot program run by universities with private funds. Any trial must first be approved by federal oversight agencies, however.

Giving heroin to addicts is unethical and can result in euthanasia. Instead of embracing the tough-love drug court approach of coercing addicts into life-saving treatment, "harm reductionists" want to keep judgment-impaired addicts in their deadly lifestyle until they die or quit by chance.

America should focus anti-drug efforts on a balanced model of enforcement, abstinence-based treatment and prevention.

Organizations to Contact

The editors have compiled the following list of organizations concerned with the issues debated in this book. The descriptions are derived from materials provided by the organizations. All have publications or information available for interested readers. The list was compiled on the date of publication of the present volume; the information provided here may change. Be aware that many organizations take several weeks or longer to respond to inquiries, so allow as much time as possible.

American Council for Drug Education
136 E. 64th St., New York, NY 10163
(800) 488-3784•fax (212) 758-6784
website: www.acde.org

The American Council for Drug Education informs the public about the harmful effects of abusing drugs and alcohol. It publishes educational materials, reviews, and scientific findings and develops educational media campaigns. The council's pamphlets, monographs, films, and other teaching aids address educators, parents, physicians, and employees.

Canadian Centre on Substance Abuse (CCSA)
75 Albert St., Suite 300, Ottawa, Ontario K1P 5E7. CANADA
(613) 235-4048•fax: (613) 235-8101
e-mail: admin@ccsa.ca•website: www.ccsa.ca

Established in 1988 by an Act of Parliament, CCSA works to minimize the harm associated with the use of alcohol, tobacco, and other drugs. It disseminates information on the nature, extent, and consequences of substance abuse; sponsors public debates on the topic; and supports organizations involved in substance abuse treatment, prevention, and education programming. The center publishes the newsletter *Action News* six times a year.

Cato Institute
1000 Massachusetts Ave., NW, Washington, DC 20001-5403
(202) 842-0200

The institute is a public policy research foundation dedicated to limiting the control of government and to protecting individual liberty. Cato, which strongly favors drug legalization, publishes the *Cato Journal* three times a year and the *Cato Policy Report* bimonthly.

Committees of Correspondence
11 John St., Room 506, New York, NY 10038
(212) 233-7151•fax: (212) 233-7063

The Committes of Correspondence is a national coalition of community groups that campaign against drug abuse among youth by publishing data about drugs and drug abuse. The coalition opposes drug legalization and advocates treatment for drug abusers. Its publications include the quarterly *Drug*

73

Abuse Newsletter, the periodic *Drug Prevention Resource Manual*, and related pamphlets, brochures, and article reprints.

Drug Enforcement Administration (DEA)
700 Army Navy Dr., Arlington, VA 22202
(202) 307-1000
website: www.usdoj.gov/dea/

The DEA is the federal agency charged with enforcing the nation's drug laws. The agency concentrates on stopping the smuggling and distribution of narcotics in the United States and abroad. It publishes the *Drug Enforcement Magazine* three times a year.

Drug Policy Foundation
4455 Connecticut Ave. NW, Suite B500, Washington, DC 20008-2328
(202) 537-5005•fax: (202) 537-3007
e-mail: dpf@dpf.org•website: www.dpf.org

The foundation supports the creation of drug policies that respect individual rights, protect community health, and minimize the involvement of the criminal justice system. It supports legalizing many drugs and increasing the number of treatment programs for addicts. Publications include the bimonthly *Drug Policy Letter* and the book *The Great Drug War*. It also distributes *Press Clips*, an annual compilation of newspaper articles on drug legalization issues, as well as legislative updates.

Heritage Foundation
214 Massachusetts Ave. NE
Washington, DC 20008-2302
(202) 546-4400

The Heritage Foundation is a conservative public policy research institute that opposes the legalization of drugs and advocates strengthening law enforcement to stop drug abuse. It publishes position papers on a broad range of topics, including drug issues. Its regular publications include the monthly *Policy Review*, the Backgrounder series of occasional papers, and the Heritage Lecture series.

Join Together
441 Stuart St., 7th Floor, Boston, MA 02116
(617) 437-1500•fax: (617) 437-9394
e-mail: info@jointogether.org•website: www.jointogether.org

Founded in 1991, Join Together supports community-based efforts to reduce, prevent, and treat substance abuse. It publishes community action kits to facilitate grassroots efforts to increase awareness of substance abuse issues as well as a quarterly newsletter.

Lindesmith Center
400 W. 59th St. New York, NY 10019
(212) 548-0695•fax: (212) 548-4670
website: www.lindesmith.org

The Lindesmith Center is a policy research institute that focuses on broadening the debate on drug policy and related issues. The center houses a library and information center; organizes seminars and conferences; acts as a link between scholars, government, and the media; directs a grant program in Europe; and undertakes projects on topics such as methadone policy reform and alternatives to drug testing in the workplace. The center publishes fact sheets on topics such as needle and syringe availability, drug prohibition and the U.S. prison system, and drug education.

Narcotic Educational Foundation of America (NEFA)
5055 Sunset Blvd., Los Angeles, CA 90027
(213) 663-5171

The NEFA provides educational materials on the dangers of drug use and abuse. It maintains a library specializing in drug abuse topics, and its publications include *Get the Answers—An Open Letter to Youth* and *Some Things You Should Know About Prescription Drugs.*

National Center on Addiction and Substance Abuse at Columbia University (CASA)
152 W. 57th St., 12th Floor, New York, NY 10019
(212) 841-5200•fax (212) 956-8020
website: www.casacolumbia.org

CASA is a private nonprofit organization that works to educate the public about the costs and hazards of substance abuse and the prevention and treatment of all forms of chemical dependency. The center supports treatment as the best way to reduce chemical dependency. It produces publications describing the harmful effects of alcohol and drug addiction and effective ways to address the problem of substance abuse.

National Institute on Drug Abuse (NIDA)
U.S. Department of Health and Human Services
5600 Fishers Ln., Rockville, MD 20857
website: www.nida.nih.gov

NIDA supports and conducts research on drug abuse—including the yearly Monitoring the Future Survey—to improve addiction prevention, treatment, and policy efforts. It publishes the bimonthly *NIDA Notes* newsletter, the periodic *NIDA Capsules* fact sheets, and a catalog of research reports and public education materials such as *Marijuana: Facts for Teens.*

Bibliography

Books

Dan Baum — *Smoke and Mirrors: The War on Drugs and the Politics of Failure*. Boston: Little, Brown, 1996.

Richard Friman — *Narco-Diplomacy: Exporting the U.S. War on Drugs*. New York: Cornell University Press, 1996.

Martin Grapendaal, Ed Leuw, and Hans Nelson — *A World of Opportunities: Life-Style and Economic Behavior of Heroin Addicts in Amsterdam*. Albany: State University of New York Press, 1995.

Mike Gray — *How We Got into This Mess and How We Can Get Out*. New York: Random House, 1999.

Arthur Herscovitch — *Everything You Need to Know About Drug Abuse*. New York: Rosen, 1998.

Ann Holmes — *The Mental Effects of Heroin*. Philadelphia: Chelsea House, 1999.

James A. Inciardi and Lana D. Harrison, eds. — *Heroin in the Age of Crack-Cocaine*. Newark: University of Delaware Press, 1999.

Mary Ann Littell — *Heroin Drug Dangers*. Springfield, NJ: Enslow, 1999.

Ann Marlowe — *How to Stop Time: Heroin from A to Z*. New York: Basic Books, 1999.

Michael Massing — *The Fix*. New York: Simon & Schuster, 1998.

Kathryn Meyer and Terry Parssinen — *Smugglers, Warlords, Spies, and the History of International Drug Trade*. New York: Rowman and Littlefield, 1999.

Richard Lawrence Miller — *Drug Warriors and Their Prey: From Police Power to Police State*. Westport, CT: Praeger, 1996.

Leif Roderick — *America's Drug War Debacle*. Aldershot, UK: Avebury, Rosenberger, 1996.

Paul B. Stares — *Global Habit: The Drug Problem in a Borderless World*. Washington, DC: Brookings Institute, 1996.

Brenda L. Underhill and Dana Finnegan — *Chemical Dependency: Women at Risk*. New York: Haworth Press, 1996.

Periodicals

Jane Adams — "My Child on Heroin? Impossible!" *New Choices*, April 1997.

Maggie Brennan   "Stopping AIDS in Its Tracks," *Mademoiselle*, June 1996.

John Cloud   "A Way Out for Junkies?" *Time*, January 19, 1998.

Henry Pierson Curtis   "A Deadly Drug, a New Generation," *Reader's Digest*, July 1998.

Jeff Elliott   "Drug Prevention Placebo: How DARE Wastes Time, Money, and Police," *Reason*, March 1995.

David France   "Heather Does Heroin," *Glamour*, September 1998.

Tom Friend   "Teens and Drugs: Today's Youth Just Don't See the Dangers," *USA Today*, August 21, 1996.

T. Trent Gegax and   "Heroin High," *Newsweek*, February 1, 1999.
Sarah Van Bouen

Richard Jerome   "The Damage Done," *People Weekly*, November 4, 1996.

Gina Kolata   "Experts Are at Odds on How Best to Tackle Rise in Teenagers' Drug Use," *New York Times*, September 18, 1996.

Rich Lowry   "Our Hero, Heroin," *National Review*, October 28, 1996.

Robert J. Maccoun   "Does Europe Do It Better? Lessons from Holland,
and Peter Reuter   Britain, and Switzerland," *Nation*, September 20, 1999.

Barry R. McCaffrey   "Prevention Programs Work," *Vital Speeches of the Day*," November 15, 1996.

Ethan Nadelmann and   "Doing Methadone Right," *Public Interest*, September 1996.
Jennifer McNeely

Sally L. Satel   "Opiates for the Masses," *Wall Street Journal*, June 8, 1998.

Karen Schoemer   "Rockers, Models, and the New Allure of Heroin," *Newsweek*, August 26, 1996.

Maia Szalavitz   "Clean Needles Saved My Life," *New York Times*, June 8, 1996.

U.S. News &   "Ignoring the Solution: Jury's In: Needle Exchanges Slow
World Report   the Spread of HIV," January 6, 1997.

David Whitman   "The Youth 'Crisis,'" *U.S. News & World Report*, May 5, 1997.

Mortimer B.   "Great Idea for Ruining Kids," *U.S. News & World*
Zuckerman   *Report*, February 24, 1997.

Index